MY NEXT STEP

An Extraordinary Journey
of Healing and Hope

─────────── DEDICATION ───────────

This book is dedicated to all those who are facing a major challenge and need to pick up the pieces and start over.

• People like wounded warriors, whose sacrifice is unlike any other.
• People battling a life-threatening disease or life-changing injury.
• People struggling with the loss of a child, a parent or any loved one.
• People experiencing a bankruptcy, failure or tragedy that makes every day difficult.

If my personal experience taught me anything, it's that each of us, with the help of others, can find a way to accept our circumstances, face the future, do what's necessary, and return to a meaningful life.

The courage to do that is within us all.

─────────────────────────────

MY

NEXT

STEP

*An Extraordinary Journey
of Healing and Hope*

BY **DAVE LINIGER**
WITH **LAURA MORTON**

HAY HOUSE, INC.
Carlsbad, California • New York City
London • Sydney • Johannesburg
Vancouver • Hong Kong • New Delhi

Library of Congress Control Number: 2013932622

ISBN: 978-1-4019-4341-7

16 15 14 13   4 3 2 1
1st edition, April 2013

Printed in the United States of America

TABLE OF CONTENTS

INTRODUCTION

I was at the 35th annual RE/MAX of Texas Statewide Convention in Galveston on January 28, 2012, to deliver a speech forecasting housing-industry trends. It was supposed to be a quick stop before heading to Boca Raton for a regional owners meeting the next day. My wife Gail was in Orlando buying golf wear and other merchandise for the pro shop at Sanctuary, the private golf club we own in Colorado. She and I had planned to meet up in Florida as soon as I was done in Galveston.

Margaret Kelly, the CEO of RE/MAX, who has been with the company more than twenty-five years, was traveling with me. She was there to speak at the same event.

Gail and I founded RE/MAX in 1973 with the simple notion of giving the very best real estate agents a full slate of support services and one hundred percent of the commission they earned instead of the fifty-fifty split they usually retained at the time. The idea was to build a company where great people could pull together to do great things. At the time, every leader in the industry told me my business platform would never work—that the financial model defied how things were done. They warned me I'd be driven out of the business before I could ever get it off the ground—that the company would *never* survive.

Fortunately, I wasn't the kind of man who was afraid to roll up my sleeves and do whatever it took to create my own success.

Hard work didn't scare me any more than my critics did. No job was beneath me, especially in the early years. I spent plenty of long nights stuffing envelopes, polishing presentations and hand-folding thousands of flyers. I look back at those grass-roots beginnings and smile at the memory of my fearlessness to face any challenge that came my way. It wasn't easy, as there were lots of challenges over the years. You see, when you've worked in real estate as long as I have, you know that the business is full of cycles. Some years are up, others down. The good and the great among us are separated by how we navigate the lean years—and believe me, there were many times along the way when I didn't know how we'd make payroll, let alone how I'd put food on the table for my own family.

Forty years later though, RE/MAX is the world's most productive real estate sales force, with roughly 90,000 agents and 6,300 offices in over 85 countries. At our peak, we had more than 100,000 agents. Our agent count dropped to roughly 85,000 during the economic downturn, but it's once again on the upswing. I look forward to having a big party when we reach the 100,000-agent milestone for the second time, as I know we will. Nothing makes me happier than having fun with my friends and colleagues—just like the many good times I've already enjoyed with them throughout our careers.

Although the real estate market took a heavy hit when the housing crisis occurred back in 2007, we persevered and found a way to navigate our way through those murky and tumultuous times. I saw the writing on the wall early enough to become instrumental in advising key players in the U.S. Treasury Department and the U.S. Department of Housing and Urban Development, recommending procedures that helped streamline the "short sale" process for distressed properties, a broadly recognized drag on the housing industry and national economy as a whole. Doing this firmly established RE/MAX as the "go to" company for those in need, keeping our business flowing and inventory moving. I don't worry about making ends meet as much as I used to, but I still spend many days and nights wondering about and calculating each careful next step, because you never know where life will lead you.

Just before leaving for Texas on that winter day, I felt as if my back was on the verge of giving out again. I'd been having terrible back problems since April 2010. My doctors had told me that some of my pain was due to being a little heavy for my frame and some of it was due to how I had treated my body over the years. Although I love to play golf, the reality is I'm not very good at it. Twisting my body to swing a club hadn't helped my back issues any more than all of the daredevil stunts I'd participated in for years. I've always considered myself to be a really tough son of a bitch and admittedly went out of my way to prove it to the world. In 1998, I trained with a team of NASA experts in the hope of sailing a specially designed and highly technologically advanced helium balloon around the world. Although we didn't make it, we sure had fun trying! As an auto-racing enthusiast, I had also completed the twenty-four hour sports car endurance race at Daytona, subjecting my body to as many as four G's around every turn along the way. I'd parachuted out of planes and faced down near-certain death on my more than 35 big game hunts in Africa and other exotic locations around the world. Some might call that need for adventure crazy—I simply called it fun.

But when my back problems became unbearable, I went to see Dr. Chad J. Prusmack, a local neurosurgeon in Denver, the city I've called home for most of my life. I knew of him because two of my officers at RE/MAX had seen him for their ailments, and because he had a terrific reputation.

When I first met Dr. Prusmack, I was surprised by how young, handsome and physically fit he is. I wanted to hate him for his good looks, but instead I admired how smart he was and took comfort in knowing that I would be in good hands if I ever needed his services. When we met in 2010, he showed me that my L5, L6 and S1 vertebrae, located at the bottom of the tailbone, had become arthritic and worn out. Dr. Prusmack explained that I had pounded the hell out of them during the years with all of the crazy and daring things I'd done to abuse my back.

"At some point, Dave, we will have to go in and work on those," he said.

Because I didn't get a sense of urgency from him, I dismissed the suggestion, thinking privately, *these doctors usually get paid to cut.* I surely wasn't ready to go under the knife anytime soon and it was so refreshing to meet a doctor who didn't want to put me through a surgery until it was absolutely necessary. That really earned my respect.

"Dave, I don't want to operate if we don't have to," he assured me. "We might be able to put it off for another year or two by giving you steroid shots in your spine to control the pain."

That was just fine with me.

Dr. Prusmack set me up with his hospital's pain center right away. The procedure was quick and easy. I was given a sedative, hooked up to an IV to repress the pain and was then given multiple shots to my spine. While the first round helped me feel about eighty percent better, there were still times when I was really suffering. This routine continued every couple of months during the next two years as a way of reducing and managing the distress I was feeling and to help me keep moving at my usual lightning-speed pace without missing a step. The last time I went into the pain center to have the shots I was feeling especially tough. I stupidly told the doctor that I didn't want the sedatives he usually administered. He looked at me like I was nuts.

"I have a high threshold for pain," I said with tremendous bravado, insisting that he just give me the shot to my spine.

I was wrong about that. *Very* wrong.

I was in agony for at least five minutes. It felt as if an electric shock was shooting straight down from my back to my left leg. It was as if I had touched a live spark plug. Not fun at all, and certainly not recommended!

"C'mon, tough guy…" the doctor coaxed until the excruciating stinging in my back finally subsided to a tolerable, but still uncomfortable, level. Once the throbbing stopped, I was completely pain free—not only had the burn from the shot eased, but my constant back pain had gone away too. The funny thing about back pain is that most people learn to live with it. Only after it's gone do you realize how much pain you were actually in. For the first time in two years, I felt great.

From that day on, I went about my life as usual. At my doctor's suggestion, I started to do some back-stretches in the morning to help keep my body limber and even lifted weights to sustain my physique and strength. As a precaution, I carried my medical records in my briefcase everywhere I went just in case anything happened while I was on the road. All I'd have to do in that event is hand the file to the attending physicians in the emergency room and they'd immediately know what we were dealing with. I remained well prepared, did all of the things I was supposed to do, and never looked back—that is, until my trip to Galveston.

I'd gotten pretty good at knowing when I was on the brink of a setback by then, and I just couldn't shake the feeling that something was about to give on the day I left Denver. The last thing I said to my secretary before boarding my plane was, "Call Dr. Prusmack and make an appointment for when I return. I think the pain meds are wearing off." I popped a couple of Aleve on board the flight and tried not to give it another thought.

We touched down in Galveston in the early afternoon of January 27th. The event was taking place at the Moody Gardens Hotel, Spa and Convention Center, which also housed an environmental museum, so I took a tour to kill some time. I've always had an interest in the environment—so much so that I helped to build The Wildlife Experience Museum in Denver, an educational, entertaining and unique blend of interactive exhibits, large format films, fine art, natural history and community outreach programs connecting visitors with many kinds of wildlife and habitats.

Later that night, Margaret and I had dinner with Richard Filip and his wife Jeanne. Richard and Jeanne are good friends of mine who at the time owned the RE/MAX of Texas region. They are very nice people, and I enjoy spending time with them whenever I'm in their area. Sometime toward the end of dinner, Jeanne and I got into a conversation about how much we hate hospitals. We both agreed that we'd rather die of an instant heart attack than spend any significant time in a hospital.

After a terrific evening, we all said goodnight and headed back to our respective hotel rooms. On the way to my suite, I turned to Margaret and said, "You know, I'm really feeling like my back is going to go out tonight. I'm going to leave my door unlocked just in case—at least you can get in to help me if I need anything." I actually placed one of my shoes on the floor between the door and the jamb to play it safe.

I'm the kind of man who rarely, if ever, asks for help. In my mind, real men don't need a hand from anyone—ever. In fact, I rather despised the thought of being dependent on someone else, so for me to suggest that I might be in need was actually a very big deal. I just had a gut feeling that something bad was about to happen.

Before I went to bed that night I also thought about the safety latch on the door that led from my room to the hotel hallway. I began to wonder, *If someone had to get in through that entry, even with a room key, would leaving it in the locked position bar them from doing so?* Just for peace of mind, I got up, unlocked it and went to sleep sometime close to ten o'clock.

Around two in the morning I awoke to find that I couldn't move my feet. I pulled the sheets off my body and stared at my legs, willing them to move, but they wouldn't budge even an inch. I physically lifted one with my hands and immediately thought, "This can't be good."

In the mid-1970s I'd had a spinal injection prior to knee surgery that left me temporarily paralyzed from the waist down during the procedure, so I was familiar with the feeling I was having and wasn't the least bit panicked about it. While I suspected it was a fluke, I did think that I should probably get myself to the local hospital.

Not wanting to disturb anyone in the middle of the night, I took my phone from the nightstand and sent text messages to Richard, Margaret and Charles El-Moussa—a RE/MAX of Texas senior officer—saying, "My back has gone out and I have to go to the hospital. When you get up in the morning would you call or come to my room?"

I spent the next several hours watching the clock tick one minute at a time. I grabbed the television remote and began flipping channels as a distraction. I don't remember watching anything in particular—just incessantly clicking from one show to the next.

Around five o'clock, I sent a text to my eldest son Dave Jr., who we all call *Junior*, to see how his night was going. Even though it was an hour earlier in Denver where he lives, I knew he'd answer.

"My night was good—how are you?" he responded.

"My back really hurts and I can't move my legs."

"Can you reach the phone in your room to dial 911?"

"No. But I've sent messages to Margaret, Richard and Charles to come get me when they wake up."

Since I'd had chronic back problems for such a long time, it wasn't unusual for me to say I was in pain. I certainly hadn't lost feeling in my legs before, but I assumed it had to be a nerve and therefore a temporary condition. I wasn't alarmed yet and the last thing I wanted to do was worry anyone else, so I stayed cool. At exactly two minutes after seven that morning, the exterior door to my room swung open. It was the hotel manager along with Charles and Richard. They didn't even knock. Just then, Margaret came through the door too.

Before anyone could say a word I looked at the gathered group and calmly said, "I'm paralyzed and cannot move my legs at all. Let's get an ambulance and get me to the nearest hospital. Back door only—no lights, no sirens. Got it?"

Even though I was in a lot of pain, I was able to think clearly and be precise about my plan. I didn't want anyone from RE/MAX who wasn't already in my room to see me going out on a stretcher. There were 1800 agents gathered at a continental breakfast that morning and I didn't need them to see me in this condition or spread the word that something was wrong. I especially didn't want a blown-out back to appear as something much worse.

I convinced Margaret to take over for me and give the speech I had prepared for the group. As they say, "The show must go on." And so it did. She stayed back and handled the event while the ambulance whisked me away.

By the time I arrived at the hospital that morning, I was in excruciating pain. Still, I pulled my medical records from my briefcase and handed them to the attending physician in the ER.

"This is probably what's happening," I said to the doctor. If I needed to have back surgery, I wanted to get home to Denver so my personal physicians could assess my situation and make the best decisions for my care. I was willing to stay in Galveston overnight if I had to, but I wanted to go home to get a better handle on my situation.

Once I was in a room and settled in at the hospital, I called my wife to tell her what was happening. I didn't want to unnecessarily worry Gail without knowing more details. To be fair, the hospital had given me large doses of painkillers, so I'm not even sure I was making a lot of sense when we spoke. I was coherent enough to ask her to leave the conference she was attending in Orlando early and to come get me with the corporate jet. I didn't want to take a medical airplane—I wanted one I was familiar with and comfortable in.

Since I was on such heavy medication, the exact events of the day remain blurry. I still didn't have a clue about what was happening to my body, but I was absolutely certain about one thing: The pain had become unbearable. Several hours later, the doctors in Galveston agreed to release me from their hospital so I could return home to be examined by my own physicians. I was unable to walk on my own. It took several people to carry me from the wheelchair to the car and then onto the waiting plane. I don't remember much except for the pain. Although I initially thought I'd find comfort on one of the aircrafts I was used to traveling on, there was no comfort to be had. I tried lying down on the floor, reclining in a chair and even leaning over the top of one of the seats. There was no relief—just unrelenting anguish.

CHAPTER 1

Unforeseen Horizons

When we landed in Denver, Junior was at the airport to meet us. He's the eldest of my four children: Dave, Mary, Chuck and John. Chuck lives in St. Augustine, Florida, so we don't get to see him as often as we see the others, who live near Gail and me in Denver.

I think Junior knew I was in a lot of pain because I usually refuse to get into one of his cars. There's no good reason for that insolence other than we are both car enthusiasts and I like my vehicles more than his. But on this particular day I wasn't picky about how I was getting home as long as I was getting there quickly. Despite my fast deteriorating condition, I told my son I didn't want to go straight to the hospital—I preferred being in the comfort of my own bed.

"We'll go tomorrow," I said, agreeing to let him take me first thing in the morning after breakfast...*if* I was still in pain. Somehow I was still hoping that this would pass—or at the very least, subside to a somewhat more manageable level of pain.

Everyone was pleading with me to go to Sky Ridge Medical Center, because it's such a great facility and very close to home, but I didn't want to be there overnight. Besides, the hospital in Galveston had already given me large doses of pain medication. *Maybe I would just sleep this off, I reasoned.* My reluctance was nothing more than sheer stubbornness and, looking back, stupidity.

Junior accompanied me to the house to make sure I was safe before heading back to his own home.

Sleep that night was completely out of the question. I couldn't move, turn over or lift my legs half an inch off the ground without assistance. The only way I could make myself comfortable was to lay flat or to pull my knees straight to my chest and prop three or four pillows underneath my calves. When I was in that position, the pain went away but the paralysis persisted. I tried not to think too much about what that meant in the long term. I was simply focused on finding a comfortable position.

JUNIOR

The first inclination I had that something was off with my dad was during a boys' golf trip to Phoenix that we'd taken a week before he fell ill. Dad likes to be warm all of the time so even though it was a pleasant sixty degrees outside, he was wearing a sweater. By the second hole though, he was complaining that he was hot. I'd never heard him say he was hot—ever. When we finished our round of golf, I took a photo of him to commemorate our day. When I saw the picture, I could tell that he didn't look right. He was struggling to stand up straight and his body was crooked. The signs of something going wrong are usually present, but they don't mean much until you reflect back on them.

When Dad texted me from Texas that night, I didn't think he was in real trouble. I knew that most of his back problems were triggered from being on a plane or even from twisting his body while playing golf. Still, I texted Margaret as soon as I heard the news because I wanted to make sure he was really ok. About an hour later, she texted back saying Dad was heading to the hospital.

When they arrived back in Denver, I could see that Dad was in terrible shape. I begged him to go to the hospital that night, but he wouldn't do it. I was relieved when he agreed to go the following morning. I really thought he'd put up a fight because my dad could usually tough out whatever pain he had. This time was different, though. Of course, looking back, I couldn't possibly know that he'd be up against the biggest battle of his life

By four o'clock that Sunday morning, less than forty-eight very long hours after I first discovered my paralysis, I finally caved in to the agony. I sent Ted, our house manager who lives with us, a text to come get me out of bed. It was apparent that I needed help, but I wasn't ready to acknowledge that it was time to go to the emergency room.

Ted immediately contacted Junior to let him know what was happening, with the hope that he could talk some sense into his old man.

Junior showed up in record time looking like he'd just rolled out of bed—which he had. When he arrived, I was sitting in a chair in our family room, wincing and groaning. He sat down next to me and said, "You're hurting bad, aren't you, Dad?"

"Yes." Frankly, there was no point in hiding the suffering. I finally admitted how bad I felt.

"You know, Dad, you've got health insurance you've been paying for years and you've hardly ever used it. Let's go down to the emergency room to let them check you out. They'll probably just give you a shot for the pain and send you home." Junior was doing his best to convince me to do the right thing—and it worked. "It's time. Let's go." There was zero reluctance in my voice.

When we got to the emergency room, I was put in a staging area where I told the attending physicians that I was having severe back pain and needed medication for it. The team there was very attentive and kind. The first doctor I saw noticed that the color of my skin was a little off and that I was having trouble breathing. He gave me the same sedatives I'd been given in Galveston to take the edge off. The doctor felt it would be better for me to be transported from the ER to a regular hospital room that morning so they could run some additional tests.

Knowing I'd likely put up a fight, Junior took my doctor aside and asked whether it would be better for me to spend the night there or go home to rest. The doctor felt it would be much better for me to stay there until they were certain about what we were dealing with.

Although I wanted to keep my condition under the radar, several friends, colleagues and family members had gathered at the hospital within hours of my arrival to keep Gail, Junior and me company while the doctors ran a battery of tests. Chuck, Mary and John were told I was going to the hospital for back pain, which wasn't anything to be alarmed about. Junior remained in constant touch with his brothers and sister, providing updates throughout the day.

They had me in a very nice room on the sixth floor—one that resembled a suite at the Four Seasons more than a hospital room. Those rooms are a little more expensive than the other rooms in the hospital, but for me, they're worth the extra price. Sky Ridge is a first-class modern facility with every comfort and amenity a patient could wish for to make a stay pleasant—even enjoyable, as strange as that may sound. The section of the hospital I was in gives new meaning to "hospital food," offering filet mignon instead of the usual I'm-not-sure-this-is-really-steak surprise you find at many places, and other fine meals cooked to order. If you want someone to stay the night with you, they will fold out a bed from the sofa in your room and make it up for your guest. It's first class all the way. If you're going to be sick, this is the place to be.

When I first got to Sky Ridge, the doctors weren't totally convinced that my paralysis and pain was exclusive to my pre-existing back problems. The doctors and nurses on duty came in and out of my room, drawing blood and running a battery of tests. I remember being told they wanted to do an MRI, but I have no recollection of it taking place because they had administered heavy-duty sedatives to keep me comfortable and still. There were several times when I felt as if I was falling into the rabbit hole as I slipped in and out of consciousness.

The last thing I strongly remember from that first day is the love and support I felt as everyone gathered in my room, keeping me company while we anxiously awaited the results of my tests. The group included RE/MAX friends like Margaret; Adam Contos, a former police officer who's now a Vice President; Vinnie Tracey, our President, who's been with us for thirty five years; and Bruce Benham, one of my senior officers, who's been with us for twenty years. They're just some of the people who were there from the very start, and they remained by my family's side throughout this ordeal. Many of my good friends from outside of RE/MAX were there too, including Dan Predovich, Chris Mauter, Dave Fisher, John Metcalf, and Bob Fisher, who was with RE/MAX from the very start but retired in the 1990s. Everyone's care and concern overwhelmed me and brought great comfort to my family.

Day turned into night. Eventually, everyone except Junior went home. He stayed by my side that night so I wouldn't be alone. He began sending updates to my other kids as well as emails to close family friends to let each of them know I was in the hospital for my back and would likely be there until Dr. Prusmack could see me the next day.

This is the part of my story where others have filled in the details for me. Many of the events that took place over the course of the next seventy-five days are reflected through their eyes and experiences. I have very little personal recollection of all that transpired, but I've been given enough information by them to piece together and share my story with you.

MARY

My brother Dave emailed me that Dad was on the sixth floor at Sky Ridge, getting a Cortisone shot for his back. I, of course, asked, "Can I come by for a visit?" I thought, sixth floor, Sky Ridge, can't be too serious, but I wanted to be by his and Gail's side. I went to the hospital late in the day on Monday—the day after he checked in— thinking he'd be lying in bed with friends all around him. But when I walked into his room, I realized something was terribly wrong. Dad was hallucinating and shaking while complaining about being hot, then cold. It was the first time in my life that I was scared for someone in my family—especially my dad, who is the toughest man I know. I wasn't prepared to see him in such a vulnerable position, but I didn't tell anyone how I really felt—which was terrified. I certainly didn't want to escalate the situation with my own emotions.

Around two o'clock that Monday morning, I began mumbling something about how many ribs we needed to make per person for the party. Gail and I had been planning our annual Super Bowl bash the following weekend, so maybe that's what was on my mind, but under the circumstances, it made no sense. Junior thought I was just talking in my sleep from all of the medication I was on and laughed off my drug-induced babble at first. But then he noticed that my breathing was becoming noticeably shallow and thought I might be taking a turn for the worse. The doctors decided to insert a ventilator tube to help me breathe. I have a gag reflex issue so it was clear that I wasn't going to tolerate their efforts well. Even when I visit the dentist, it takes a lot of nitrous oxide and some good Doors music on my headphones to make me relaxed enough to sit still in the chair. It's a good thing I was in a semi-conscious state, because they wouldn't have been able to get that tube in any other way.

By Monday afternoon, Mary and John arrived at Sky Ridge to see me. John immediately recognized that I was having a very hard time getting out of bed to go to the bathroom, and suggested that the doctors insert a catheter to keep me more comfortable and still. My paralysis made it all but impossible to stand on my own, so as painful as it was to insert, it was the best solution for when nature called. John has a wonderful understanding of critical medical issues and is very tuned in to information of that sort. He grew up with a hereditary condition that I am a carrier of, called Factor 5 DNA, which means we have a propensity for blood clots. As a result, John has spent many years studying blood. He also had a girlfriend who sustained a spinal injury in a terrible car accident, so he had heard much of what the doctors were talking about regarding my back issues before. With all of this knowledge, he became an instant advocate for me, not just as my son, but also as someone who had enough understanding and experience dealing with hospitals to be an effective liaison for the family. He could talk to the doctors in a language they both understood, taking in each morsel of information and giving it meaning for everyone else who couldn't grasp the severity of what was really happening. He could also suggest alternative treatments that the doctors might not have considered. I'm told he was a significant factor in making sure I was medically well taken care of early on.

Sometime late on Monday, Junior suddenly noticed blood in my urine bag. He didn't have the same medical background as John, but he knew enough to understand that blood in the urine meant my kidneys could be failing. Shortly after that, my kidneys did completely shut down. The doctors put me on dialysis right away, but this development worsened my condition to critical. My body was quickly giving way to whatever was happening inside, which still remained a deep mystery to us all.

From the time I arrived at Sky Ridge, my body temperature was steadily over one hundred degrees, sometimes spiking upwards of one hundred and four. This was a sure sign that in addition to my back issues, I was fighting some type of infection. I had been traveling a lot prior to getting sick and my body was severely fatigued. I'd been on planes and in hotel rooms all over the country for several weeks at a time. I was physically and mentally exhausted, which wasn't exactly helping my body battle off potential germs. Even with these fluctuations, by the time Tuesday morning came, I had stabilized enough to give Junior the confidence to go home, take a shower, walk his dogs and get a little sleep. I don't think he closed his eyes once in my hospital room during those first two nights. He had to be on the verge of exhaustion himself.

Since my children were working in shifts those first few days, John and my good friend Adam took over when Junior left that morning. That's when one of the doctors on duty noticed that my urine now had an unusual cloudy appearance. He tested it, suspecting that something much bigger was brewing than just a back issue. Around seven-thirty that morning, he called John over to look at the results of the test. He said there was some type of severe infection in my body that was becoming rampant. He wasn't sure what it was, but he was positive it was quickly spreading and shutting down my organs. He strongly suggested that I be moved to the ICU as soon as possible. John didn't hesitate in making that decision. He was educated enough to see that there was a real problem growing by the minute. Knowing his siblings would agree, he approved that decision on the spot. The doctor told him it was obvious I was very ill.

JOHN

If you are the man at the trigger...you do it. I did try to include everyone in on decisions based on my previous experience, but in this instance, I just knew this was the right way to go. The doctors were very comfortable coming to me and saying, "Can you speak to the family?" because I could relay the information in language that made sense to both the doctors and my siblings in a calm and collected manner. I was a 737-captain instructor. When you are in the simulators, everything is a crisis because they don't pay you to have a smooth flight in the simulator. My girlfriend always said that I should be a crisis counselor, because for me, making decisions under pressure is so easy. And that was the role that I was supposed to play at that moment and I happened to be there.

From what I've been told, everything seemed to go into fast-forward when my urine test results came back. I was still in a semi-conscious state, so I had no way of knowing what was happening. I fell asleep in the comfort of my suite and awoke in the ICU. I was disoriented, confused and too drugged up to comprehend that I was likely dying. There was a lot of scurrying around, which made everyone nervous. While I was being transferred, John and Adam sent a text to Junior to get him back to the hospital as soon as possible. They sensed that decisions were going to have to be made quickly.

JUNIOR

By the time I arrived back to the hospital on Tuesday morning, Dad was already in the ICU. Things had really taken a sharp turn for the worse. It was obvious that the doctors had a new sense of urgency they didn't have when I left that morning. They were spending more time behind the desk at the nurse's station, reading Dad's files and staying quiet. Doctors never really talk to the family when they're reading through files, but it didn't take long to figure out that they were concerned. Suddenly a few new machines and a new IV drip were brought into Dad's room. I texted my brother Chuck to let him know things were getting serious. I told him it was time to get to Denver as soon as he could, as I wasn't sure Dad was going to make it.

The early stages of being in the ICU are spent trying to get the critically ill patient under control. For me, that meant heavy doses of medication for the pain, which put me in a drug-induced semi-coma. I wasn't really aware of anything happening around me. Whenever I came to, I would try to talk, but I was terribly incoherent. With the ventilator tube down my throat it was nearly impossible to speak above a whisper. Still, my first question was always the same: "How's Gail?"

The doctors said they weren't sure if I had somehow contracted spinal meningitis or something worse. They would need to perform more tests to know what they were dealing with and how to treat it. Sometimes I'd wake up and beg whoever was in the room to get me out of there. I'd plead with them to unhook the tubes and free me before falling back asleep unable to remember what happened five minutes before that. I've never been the kind of man who likes to feel confined. Even in my altered state, I had enough sense to understand that I was someplace I didn't want to be.

The results of some blood cultures can take several days to come back, so everyone was extremely nervous as they waited for answers. With every passing hour, my organs began shutting down. When you're in shock, everything in your body can fail except your brain. You can actually comprehend that you're in danger, even if you're unconscious.

Well before going into the hospital, I had been diagnosed with type 2 diabetes. I knew I was at risk for coronary disease because I wasn't exercising as much as I should have been. In the past, I had worked out, lifted weights, climbed the rugged canyons in Lake Powell and always felt strong. But now, I'd never felt so weak or helpless.

In the midst of this, the doctors diagnosed me with high

blood pressure and atrial fibrillation, also known as a-fib (an irregular heartbeat). My heart rate was fluctuating all over the place. A normal heart rate sustains a bpm somewhere in the sixties. Mine never got below the low eighties, and sometimes went as high as one hundred eighty. It would go up and then down, causing my blood pressure to be out of control. My liver began to fail too. In all fairness, I can't say that enjoying a drink or two throughout my sixty-seven years helped much. Joking aside, these conditions were serious enough on their own. When combined with my current state, they became *extremely* dangerous. It had to be terribly disconcerting for everyone to watch my body being ravaged in this way.

When the blood cultures finally came back, the news wasn't good. Dr. Prusmack told my family that I most likely had methicillin resistant staph aureus (MRSA), a run-of-the-mill staph infection in my body that had become septic. Staph aureus is one of the five most common types of staph infections, affecting as many as half a million patients a year. One-third of us carry this type of staph in our bodies, especially in the nose, back of the throat or on the skin. Thankfully, this kind of staph infection is generally considered insignificant because it's a type of bacteria that is easily treatable with the right antibiotics.

When staph hits the body, it can migrate to your heart, lungs or bones. In my case, the infection was looking for a place to attach itself. Since I had lower back damage from prior injuries, the infection manifested itself mainly along my spine. This made my case a bit more complicated than most. The MRI images came back showing sacs of pus all along my vertebrae. When doctors conduct an MRI exam, they start at the spine and go through all four sections from your lower back to your brain stem. Each one had an abscess formation. It is not uncommon to have the infection in parts of the spine, but it is extremely rare to have it along the entire spine and into the brain stem. Worse yet, my blood tests showed that the infection had spread to my blood too, making it mobile throughout my body. I was later told this was the first time my medical team had ever seen this type of infection affect the entire spine. Although they had treated similar cases, mostly the thoracic and lumbar parts of the spine, they hadn't seen anything quite like the infection that ran along mine from top to bottom. As they say, go big or go home.

Now that the doctors were able to identify the type of staph infection I'd contracted, they could figure out the best method for treatment. They agreed that antibiotics would be their initial course of action and administered heavy doses to start reducing the presence of the pus sacs that were creating pressure on my spine. While there might be the need to perform surgery down the road, they first hoped to control the worst of the infection through the use of drugs before making the decision to perform delicate surgery that could cause permanent damage along my spine.

Now that my disease had a name, everyone was trying to figure out how I might have contracted my sepsis in the first place. As I mentioned, I traveled all of the time and slept in various hotel rooms, so it was possible that I picked it up sometime during my travels. One of the doctors also talked about several studies linking MRSA to Vietnam vets, especially those who may have been exposed to Agent Orange during the war, as I was. But then, someone in my family recalled that I had a cut on my arm that wouldn't heal for weeks. I collect cars and had recently acquired an electric car called a Tesla. It's a two-seat sports car that can go from 0-60 mph in 3.2 seconds. Even with that power, it's really like a souped up golf cart because there are no gears, and when you step on the accelerator, it makes very little noise. It's so quiet that you feel like you're driving a stealth vehicle. Like a golf cart, the Tesla has to be plugged in to be charged. I had put an extension cord on the ground of our garage, and made it a point to tell everyone to be careful not to trip over it. I meant to tape it to the floor but before I could, I forgot it was there and tripped over it myself. I landed pretty hard and though I managed to roll out of my fall, I cut my arm from my elbow down toward my wrist. The wound wasn't deep enough to need stitches but it took quite a while for it to mend completely. I didn't think much of it at the time, but looking back, that was the most likely source of my infection—a simple slip and fall in my garage!

In just a little over three days, I had gone from being a pretty healthy guy in his sixties, able to endure speeds of 218 mph with the best of them, to a quickly deteriorating old man struggling to stay alive.

CHAPTER 2

Leave No Man Behind

"Energetically will I meet the enemies of my country. I shall defeat them on the field of battle for I am better trained and will fight with all my might. Surrender is not a Ranger word. I will never leave a fallen comrade to fall into the hands of the enemy and under no circumstances will I ever embarrass my country."

The Ranger Creed
5th Stanza

For as long as I can remember, we've had a family rule to never leave a loved one alone in the hospital. I suppose I've been that way ever since I served in Vietnam, but I really became committed to that type of support after my wife, Gail, who was then my fiancée, was in a horrific plane crash back in 1983. From that time on, whenever a family member, friend or colleague was in the hospital, I always made it a point to be there, right by their side. We've all heard horror stories about what can happen when you're alone—from being given the wrong medication to needing a nurse when one isn't around because they are busy helping other patients. There is a gift your presence provides to the person who is not in control. When you're lying in a hospital bed, thoughts of the worst-case scenarios are the hardest to wipe from your mind. That's when fear creeps in. Having the presence of a friend or relative takes away the panic. No strings, no expectations—this simple offering of comfort, assuring them that they aren't alone, helps in ways that cannot be measured.

In October 1983, Gail and I were in Canada for a RE/MAX International conference. RE/MAX was only ten years old and growing fast. We were quickly becoming one of the most powerful real estate brands in the world. Gail and I were fully committed to our company, making sacrifices to realize our dreams. We were on the road five days a week, sometimes longer, selling new franchises while strengthening and expanding our relationships with existing territories. We were both workaholics who found more satisfaction in helping others reach their career goals than we did most anything else—except each other. Gail and I were engaged to be married the following month. We were on top of the world, approaching the top of the real estate game and about to start our new life together, when the unthinkable happened.

We were at the Deerhurst Resort in Huntsville, Ontario, not far from Toronto. During our stay, Frank Polzler, who co-owned RE/MAX for all of Eastern Canada, invited Gail, myself, and a mutual friend, Randy Lerum, to visit his cabin on a nearby lake. We'd have to travel by seaplane to get there. Although Gail and I were both trained pilots (Randy had helped us get our licenses!), Gail had never been on a seaplane before, so she was very excited to make the quick fifteen-minute trip from our resort to Frank's vacation home. I decided not to go because I had some business dealings I wanted to tend to with some colleagues who were waiting for me inside the resort.

It wasn't the clearest day, nor was it perfect conditions for flying, I thought to myself as I stood on the dock to watch their plane take off. To my trained eye, something seemed off as the seaplane struggled to ascend into the air. It appeared heavy and climbed a little too slow for my comfort. As it cleared the trees in the distance, I turned to walk back to the resort but had a bad feeling as I made my way up the path.

The plane had landed safely at the lake, where Gail and Frank took a quick tour before boarding for their return trip. This time however, as the plane began to accelerate for takeoff, it simply couldn't get off the ground fast enough. They were quickly headed toward the edge of the lake, where they surely wouldn't clear the trees and power lines in front of them.

Enough time had passed without Frank's plane returning to the resort that I began to worry. I called the local police stations to see if anyone had heard about a small plane crash. In my gut, I already knew the answer, but it didn't hit me until someone confirmed the worst.

"There *has* been a plane crash, sir. Some of the passengers are dead. We don't have any more information at this time."

The pilot was killed on impact, but rescue workers and Good Samaritans from the lakeside community who saw the crash were able to pull Gail, Randy and Frank from the wreckage. Frank and Randy were badly hurt, but they weren't in critical condition. Gail wasn't as lucky. Her injuries were so severe that the paramedics wanted her immediately transported to Sunnybrook Hospital in Toronto, a facility that specialized in severe trauma cases.

I raced to be by her side. By the time I got to Sunnybrook, Gail was in a coma. The doctors told me that she was not likely to survive and if she did, she might never walk again due to her brain injury. I've never been the kind of man who accepts defeat with grace and I surely wasn't about to then. That kind of dire prognosis was simply not an option. I knew Gail had the strength to not only survive this ordeal, but to find a way to walk again someday.

I had never left a man behind, and I wasn't about to start now. This is the kind of philosophy taught in the military and it has become a part of my vernacular ever since I served in the Air Force. Soldiers are trained to move hell and high water to make this statement true to the extent that it's within their power. But the truth is, sometimes people do get left behind—not on my watch however, and certainly not now.

Although Gail suffered a severe and traumatic head injury, partial paralysis on the left side of her body and several shattered bones, I was committed to doing whatever it would take to help get her through this, to keep her strength up, her motivation high and her morale bolstered so she would never think about giving up her fight.

I've always been a voracious reader, especially of motivational business books, so I spent hours, then days that ultimately turned into weeks, reading inspiring books to Gail while she lay in her hospital bed. I stayed with her twenty hours a day making sure no one spoke about the possibility of her never walking again or used any other discouraging language in her midst. Only positive messages of hope could be offered to keep her determination from wavering. When my voice became gravelly from reading, I played motivational tapes at her bedside. I constantly reassured Gail that she could beat her challenges—that she was stronger than her injuries.

Once Gail was able to, we made arrangements to transfer her back to Denver, where she would start her long and tough road to recovery. I called my closest confidants back home and asked them to help me find the very best rehabilitation hospital in the country for head injuries. I was emphatic in my desire to find the *BEST* for Gail. Even though I didn't have a lot of money back then I didn't care about the cost of her care. I would make whatever personal sacrifices necessary to ensure that Gail got the help she needed to come back from the brink of death and live a good and healthy life.

Word came back that Craig Hospital in Denver seemed to be the best place for Gail to be. This news made me angry at first because I thought everyone was simply trying to make things easier for me by picking a *local* hospital instead of actually finding her the *best* facility for her circumstances.

I was wrong.

As it turns out, Craig Hospital ranked in the top five on every list. They had a long waiting list for people to get in, but were willing to take Gail if I was willing to bring her there. I agreed to fly back with her to check it out.

We boarded a special plane equipped to transport patients who are in a lot of pain. It was a horribly bumpy flight, making the already agonizing trip nearly impossible for Gail. Her left arm was in a cast and no matter how insulated it was, every bump hurt like hell.

When we landed, an ambulance took us right to Craig, where Gail was immediately admitted as a patient. While the staff was tending to her needs, I started looking around and realized it was unlike any hospital I had ever seen before. It certainly wasn't like the hospital we had just left, where Gail spent most of her time in the intensive care unit with doctors and nurses in scrubs and wearing stethoscopes around their necks.

As I wandered around the facility, it was hard to tell who the doctors and nurses were. Everyone was dressed very casually, wearing mostly jeans and t-shirts.

"We're screwed," I thought. "Get me the hell out of this place." I was really furious. I went home that night to figure out my next step. Surely I'd have to move her to someplace better equipped with more experienced professionals. The only question was: Where?

When I returned to Craig the next morning, I stood off to the side and observed how the physical therapists and doctors were working with Gail. One of the nurses noticed me in the background.

"Everything ok, Mr. Liniger?" she asked.

"I find it strange that nobody is in scrubs or even remotely appears like they're working in a hospital." I was being candid, if not somewhat gruff and protective.

"We try everything we can to convince our patients that they are on a college campus. Most of the patients who come here are young, and they're used to wearing jeans. The majority of our nurses, therapists and technicians are young too. They spend the bulk of their days working on the floor or mats, picking people up or helping them learn to do something they once took for granted in a whole new way. We may appear casual, but the people who work here are the very best in the world. Don't judge us by the way we look. Judge us by the results we get."

Pow.

Her explanation hit me right between the eyes. It was a valuable lesson learned, one I would never forget.

A few days after arriving at Craig, the doctors told me that they needed to redo the surgery on Gail's left arm to aid in her recovery because her wrist still wasn't stabilizing. Since Craig is a rehab hospital, they sent us to another hospital in Denver to have that procedure done. Essentially, they would need to break her wrist, remove the plate that was put in at the hospital in Toronto and put a new plate in its place. Wanting the best for her, I agreed to let them do it.

Gail was taken to a nearby hospital, where a very good doctor would do the surgery. As always, I stayed right by her side. I wanted to make sure she wasn't in any unnecessary pain and didn't feel alone. I stayed in the room all night in a chair that was right behind the door. I placed a bath towel over a small clip-on book light I used to read while Gail rested. I'd go over to check on her from time to time or push the button on her morphine drip to make sure she wasn't uncomfortable and then I'd sit back down to read some more. I didn't sleep a wink that night—I couldn't.

Just before daylight broke the next morning, a doctor came into Gail's room with a nurse.

"How is she doing?" he asked the nurse.

"She's doing fine, doctor. I checked on her once an hour throughout the night," the nurse responded.

I was seeing red.

"You're a liar!" I bellowed from behind the door.

The doctor and nurse physically jumped, as they didn't know I was sitting there.

"I've sat here all night, and not one nurse has come through that door. I never left the room or fell asleep. Nobody has been in here to check on that woman since ten o'clock last night until you two just walked in." There was no hiding how mad I was and from that point on, I was on the doctors and nurses like white on rice because I suddenly realized that if I hadn't been there that night, the nurse would have told the doctor the same story but no one would have been there to be Gail's advocate. You see, when a patient is kept drugged up for pain, they have no idea what is happening to them or when it's happening. They are often unable to speak for themselves. There was absolutely no chance I'd ever potentially leave Gail or anyone I care about in that vulnerable position again.

Even though I'd adhered to the "leave no man behind" philosophy since I was in the military, this was the seminal moment when I vowed to myself that it would be my policy for life. No one deserves to be alone when they are sick, helpless and unable to care for themselves.

This point was driven home a few days later when one of Gail's doctors stopped me in the hallway.

"I hear you've been giving Gail her showers instead of letting our nursing staff do it," he said.

It's true that I had started giving Gail her showers because her room didn't have a wheelchair-accessible shower stall in it, so Gail had to be taken to another room that had the right kind of shower. I'd get her bundled up in a warm blanket and take her there myself. I lifted her out of her wheelchair and placed her into a shower chair—a special chair designed to be used by patients who cannot stand on their own. I'd get her washed, take her out, dry her hair and then wheel her back to her room, where I'd lift her into bed again. I did the same thing when she needed to go to the bathroom, too. I'd carry her from the bed to the toilet and then back again. Frankly, after the run-in with that nurse, I didn't trust Gail in anyone's hands but mine.

I wasn't really sure where the doctor was headed with our conversation.

"Well, just be careful because I've heard you've already dropped her once," the doctor said in a very condescending tone. I looked him straight in the eyes and said, "What are you talking about?" I was really angry by his accusation because there was no shred of truth to what he was saying.

"One of our technicians mentioned that you dropped Gail while carrying her to the bathroom."

"That is a total lie! The nurse dropped her. I watched her take Gail to the toilet and she turned her back for a moment and let Gail fall. Nobody will ever touch her in this hospital again. Outside of her doctors, I will be the only one to take care of Gail. Do you understand what I am saying?" I could feel the blood in my body begin to boil as I lambasted this doctor for the offensive and false accusation he was making.

It turned out that the nurse on duty who had dropped Gail wrote in her daily report that *I* had dropped her because she was afraid that if the truth came out she would lose her job. When I confronted her, she began to cry and apologized for her mistake. Look, I get that people make mistakes—we are all human. However, I was willing, ready and able to be a royal pain in the ass if it meant keeping Gail safe and secure during her recovery. I was in love with her and she was critically injured. If I couldn't be her advocate, who would be?

By the time we got back to Craig Hospital, I'd told everyone at RE/MAX that Gail was my top priority. I needed to stay by her side so nothing like this would ever happen again. We were a much smaller company at the time—just twenty-five of us in the office—but every single person stepped up to help in any way they could. Secretaries stopped at my house in the mornings to feed and walk our dog. They'd sometimes bring him into the office so he wasn't alone all of the time. Everyone played with him, threw the ball around and let him run at lunchtime. At night another group would feed and walk him or take him back to the house. Sometimes I'd take a couple of hours away from Gail so I could go home, see the dog, take a shower, open mail and nap before heading right back to the hospital. But when I did leave, I made damn sure there was always someone with Gail.

After several weeks of this routine, one of Gail's nurses took me aside and suggested that I—make that *strongly encouraged* me to—sit in on a group therapy session. I'd become friendly with this particular nurse because she was a no-nonsense woman—my favorite kind. She was direct and sincere, which I always appreciate.

"Dave, I want you to do this for me. We are treating Gail fine here, but you are still being a total pain in the ass to the staff, so I need you to go talk about your anger and frustration, ok?"

I hated to admit it, but she was right. I had gotten so caught up in taking care of Gail, keeping her safe and never turning my back on her, that I'd become very tightly wound. I was on verge of cracking, which wouldn't do anyone a bit of good, so I reluctantly and begrudgingly agreed to go.

Now, I'm not sure the rest of this story puts me in the best light, but it's honest and it's what happened.

When I got to the group therapy session, they went around the room and asked each person to tell us why they were there. The first person spoke and said, "My husband fell out of a cherry picker, and because he wasn't wearing his safety harness, he broke his neck and is paralyzed from the shoulders down."

The next person said, "I don't know what we are going to do for money. We don't have insurance and our savings have run out."

The third person spoke next: "Our son got drunk at his homecoming party and rolled his car four times. He killed his girlfriend and has a broken back. He's ruined his future and ours, because we can't afford to pay the medical bills either."

Finally, they get to me.

I sat there, clearly angry and frustrated to be in the room.

"Dave, would you like to tell us why you're here today?" The group therapist was speaking to me in a gentle tone, but all I heard was blah, blah, blah.

"I've got nothing to say. My fiancée's nurse asked me to sit through a session, so that's what I'm doing here today." I've been known to be a bit stubborn over the years. I wasn't budging and I certainly had no intention of sharing my feelings in a group full of strangers.

"Why don't you tell us how you feel, Dave?"

"My feelings are *my* feelings!" I was beginning to raise my voice, so they moved on to the next person before going around the room yet again, and then once more.

As they say, the third time's a charm. When they came back to me for the third time that day, I was ready to talk—and boy, did I.

"You want to know how I feel? Ok. I'll tell you how I feel. My fiancée has a traumatic head injury and we don't know how much she's going to come back from it. Right now she's also paralyzed on the left side of her body. Her life has changed forever. And I feel very sad for that loss. I'm angry about it. This is a wonderful woman who got hurt by no fault of her own. I'm not here to cry or bellyache and tell you all how bad I feel about our situation. I know what my next step is going to be. I'm going to get her out of this damned hospital and she is going to learn to walk. We are going to make the best life we can make with what we have left. I know it will never be the same, and I can live with that. I'm not going to talk about it anymore. It's happened, and I've put that story in a box and hid it in the back of my brain, which is where it will stay. This won't define who we are or who we'll be. I have a beautiful woman in my life. And as she heals, we're going to make a brand new life together. Can I leave this fucking meeting now?"

When Gail's nurse heard about my outburst, she smiled and said, "I'm very proud of you."

Mission accomplished.

Looking back, I realize I shouldn't have handled the group that way, but I was extremely uptight and although I wasn't aware of it at the time, was about to explode. The fact that I could look forward was a gift—not a detriment. I sat in that group therapy session and listened as each person spoke. They had no idea what their next step was going to be. They were lost and couldn't figure it out. The therapist was trying to show us that if we talked about the fear, anger, resentment or loss we were experiencing and allowed ourselves to feel our emotions, over time we'd come to grips with the situation. Then, once we did that, we could start moving forward one step at a time. I was already ten steps ahead of the others when I sat there that day, and I don't regret a word of what I said.

Life brings us unexpected happenings every day. We have the choice and the power to choose how we react to those situations and circumstances. At some point, each of us will likely face something terrible—the loss of a parent, best friend or child, a bitter divorce, or even the bankruptcy of a business. We're left to pick up the pieces. Our response to the occurrence dictates the outcome.

"Pain is inevitable. Suffering is optional."

-M. Kathleen Casey

Several years after Gail's accident, I was struck by something I read in Jack Canfield's book, *Success Principles: How to Get From Where You Are to Where You Want to Be*. It was called the E+R=O theory. Event+Response=Outcome. Canfield's book is one of the best success and motivational works that I've ever read. In the book, Canfield tells a story about a big earthquake in Southern California. Freeway overpasses buckled, city streets were torn up and commuting around LA had suddenly become a science. A reporter was in the field covering people's reactions, doing man-on-the-street interviews. The first man he stopped to talk to was sitting in his car. Traffic was at a complete stop, so the reporter knocked on the window and asked, "What do you think about this mess?"

The man in the car was a heavyset older gentleman who was clearly unhappy. "First it was the floods and then it was the gangs and now it's the damned earthquake! I HATE California. It sucks!" Veins were popping out of the sides of his neck, as his face grew red from rage.

The reporter knocked on the next car's window.

"What do you think of this mess?"

The demeanor of the man inside was drastically different. "Well, we've had an awful earthquake. The streets have fallen down and they are blocked, so it's much harder to get around the city. I get up an hour and a half earlier than I used to and it takes me almost two hours to get to work, but it's ok. I have a Thermos full of coffee, a couple of sandwiches and cookies, and am listening to tapes to help me learn to speak English a little better. It's slow going, but it is what it is. This too shall pass."

The same event happened to both men. The earthquake and traffic jams affected everyone, but one man's answer was filled with anger and hatred while the other man's answer was relaxed and accepting.

The Event–E—was the earthquake.

The Response–R—was anger versus acceptance.

The Outcome–O—was a man who was tightly wound and most likely headed for a heart attack versus another who who took the event in stride and actually used the time to improve his English.

E+R=O became a lesson I would include in many speeches going forward, especially when the housing market began to collapse.

In 2007, Margaret Kelly, Vinnie Tracey and I set out on a thirty-city speaking tour around the country to give a three-hour course on the changes in real estate that were just beginning to unravel the industry. We wanted to prepare our brokers and agents for what was coming, explore what it meant and suggest ways to respond to it. We called this our *Be Great in 2008* tour. The basic message was that everyone needed to understand the local market and respond accordingly. For many, this would require a major change to meet the new conditions. There would be no overnight fix—if your market changed, you had to change with it. We urged each and every person to stop daydreaming about things going back to the way they used to be, and to do the work necessary to adapt.

By this time, many who couldn't make it in the new economy had fallen out of the business, so the bulk of the people we were addressing were those who already had the survival mentality it took to succeed. We drew upon Jack Canfield's E+R=O theory as a way to illustrate to those agents and brokers that their response to the housing and economic crisis—and not the downturn itself—would dictate their outcome.

Were they willing to be retrained or were they determined to hang onto the memories of how easy things used to be? Would they work hard, learning how to navigate through fore-closures on distressed properties and deal with panicked sellers whose homes were upside down in value? Could they face the reality that they themselves would need to tighten their belts because fewer sales overall meant lower incomes for most? If they weren't willing to make that kind of commitment and sacrifice, it was time to get out of the business because they would never survive.

To succeed, they'd have to figure out a plan and then decide what their response would be.

Even though I didn't have the benefit of knowing about E+R=O when I was dealing with Gail's recovery, it perfectly matched my attitude at that time. She had had a terrible event, but our response to it, together, would determine the outcome of our lives going forward. And our lives were going to be great.

I would use the same formula later in my own recovery, when I lay virtually motionless in my hospital bed, thinking about the choices I faced.

Because of all we'd been through together twenty-nine years earlier, it was incredibly important to Gail that she had the chance to support me through this crisis as I had supported her.

We committed ourselves to each other many years ago—in good times and bad, in sickness and in health. A bend in the road is not the end of the road. We've had a wonderful life together, and that wasn't going to change because of my illness.

In my case, E+R=O, at least for the things I controlled, was a pretty simple formula:

E—Getting sick

R—Giving up or fighting

O—Living or dying

How I would proceed was my choice to make.

CHAPTER 3
Controlled Chaos

JUNIOR

O nce we were told that Dad could die, John, Mary and I quickly rallied as a group. Mary and I live the closest to the hospital and are the most available so we each took a twelve-hour shift ensuring that Dad would never be alone. Mary came around six o'clock in the morning and I usually arrived around six at night. Everything was happening so fast that our brother Chuck, who lives in Florida, wasn't yet aware of just how bad things had gotten. Once we filled him in, he made arrangements to be by Dad's side that same day.

The first thing we did was set up a barrier at the hospital to protect my father's privacy. The hospital placed him under VIP status with no name on record. If someone called looking for Dave Liniger, no one could unintentionally give out any personal information about his condition because he wouldn't appear as a registered patient. The answer to such callers' questions would be, "He is not a patient here" or "Contact his family."

A friend of mine, who works as a reporter for a local news station, just happened to be in the hospital that day and wanted to know why I was there. By this time, Dad was comatose. He wasn't able to speak for himself and we wanted to do everything we could to preserve his dignity. I didn't get into details with the reporter that day, but I knew she could tell something was very wrong.

Next, we sat down as a group and set some ground rules amongst ourselves. By this time my brother Chuck had arrived from Florida, so he was in on the decision making too. John, Mary, Chuck, Gail a small group of Dad's closest friends and I determined that every decision had to be unanimous. No one was empowered to make a single decision without sending a text or email to everyone else to be sure we were all on the same page.

We unanimously agreed that we wouldn't turn Dad's condition into a high-pressure situation where everyone is fighting, arguing and competing to be the person who did the most. When the stakes are this high, even the littlest things can turn a close family against one another.

Someone told us the reason they keep security in the ICU waiting room is because families explode from the pressure. It has nothing to do with stealing drugs from the pharmacy or any other crime. It's because families have a tendency to collapse on each other. We each vowed that wouldn't happen to us.

Finally, we gathered Dad's cell phone, iPad and other personal items and put them all in a safe. If, for whatever reason, Dad passed away, his privacy couldn't be intruded upon. We all agreed that if something were to happen, that's where it would stay, unopened and never to be viewed. It's not that we thought Dad had anything to hide—it's just that we all agreed that he deserved his privacy in life and if needed, in death.

JOHN

My girlfriend who was in the car accident was able to recover from her injuries, but what we were never able to recover from was the negative stuff that occurred between her family, friends and me in the waiting room. I would say, "Guys, I know what is going on here and we have to do this because it is the next logical step." It was an unfortunate experience in that the venom and the bad blood in that waiting room when she was ill had the worst impact on our relationship. I wasn't willing to go through that again with my own family, so I made sure we all stuck together as much as we could. We found a comfortable place for everyone to be and it happened to work out. It was funny because the doctors and nurses would all say the same thing—that we were an exception to the rule. Even the chaplain thought we should collaborate on creating a pamphlet for people in the ICU, sharing our advice on how to cope with the stress of the waiting room.

CHUCK

When I arrived at Sky Ridge, I was shocked to see how sick Dad was. My dad is tough—like John Wayne tough— so it was weird to see someone like him in that condition. We have a tight family, especially the kids. We are all really close with our mom and dad and our stepmom and step-dad. We talk or text each other every day. This was the first time we had a close family member in that much trouble. It was shocking.

JUNIOR

We didn't want to scare anyone outside our immediate family about Dad's condition until we knew more about it. We were all aware that there are a lot of people who rely on him, including the more than three hundred employees of RE/MAX at the corporate headquarters in Denver, The Wildlife Experience Museum, the staff at Sanctuary and so many others who worked by his side every day.

I spent half of my nights by Dad's bedside keeping a close eye on him and the other half typing out texts and email replies to everyone who couldn't get a hold of him. It wasn't unusual for me to field messages for Dad if someone was trying to reach him and couldn't. But this time was different because as hard as we tried to keep a lid on things, bad news always has a way of getting out. My usual response was to share just enough information without giving up his privacy. I'd write back, "Dad is in the hospital now and doesn't have his cell phone."

I promised that when the time was right, I'd get back to each and every person to keep them updated and if and when he got better, we'd let anyone who wanted to spend time with him have that time. In our own subtle way, it was clear to everyone we spoke to that things were serious. We were preparing for the worst and hoping for a miracle. There wasn't much else we could do except be with Dad, support him, stay positive and offer our unconditional love and support.

MARY

As a way to keep morale up, on the morning of February 5th, my brother John came up with the idea to host a Super Bowl party for all of the family and friends who had loved ones in the ICU. Sky Ridge had never allowed anything like this to happen in the ICU. We knew how hard it was for all of the families going through the same kind of traumatic experience we were—we thought it would give everyone a much needed release of tensions to watch the New England Patriots and the New York Giants battle it out to see who would win the Lombardi trophy.

We brought in a big screen TV and turned it into an ICU potluck dinner, with each of us bringing in a dish to enjoy while watching the game together as if we were in someone's home. There's nothing comfortable about the ICU waiting room and worse, you know everyone there is in crisis. There was no better way to create a much-needed camaraderie among us than to watch a good ol' football game. Even though tensions were high among the families that were there that day, every single person could breathe a little easier or simply let out a sigh of relief for those few hours. Hospital security actually showed up and asked us to keep down the noise. It's true that we were loud, but it was a day for everyone to relax.

JOHN

We weren't going to have the Super Bowl party at first because some people thought that it was disrespectful for the other people in the waiting room. But then, I happened to go into the waiting room earlier that day and people from other families asked, "Are you going to bring in the big screen TV?"

I knew every family in the ICU was struggling. We didn't want to intrude, but I genuinely thought the Super Bowl would provide a great four-hour break in the tension. "We already ordered pizzas and were planning on this," some of the other families said. "We need to escape from our reality." It was obvious they agreed with our decision, so we carried on with the plan. The staff had to tell us to keep the noise down a couple of times, but they wandered through to get the score every now and then, too.

CHUCK

I stayed by Dad's side for about a week. I picked up a nasty cold from being around the hospital. When I discussed it with the doctors, they said it would be better if I wasn't around—even in the waiting room for fear of getting anyone else sick. So, I flew back to Florida until I was healthy again. My girlfriend Bonnie and I started traveling back and forth with one of us trying to be there as often as we could throughout Dad's stay in the ICU. When I couldn't be there, I'd get constant updates. Junior and Mary were at the hospital around the clock. John personally knew many of Dad's doctors. They were all a little more in tune with the actual illnesses and what he was going through. I would ask for briefings and updates. I told every one of them that we were on the same page and in agreement. If a surgery had to be done, they had my full support for it and if they couldn't get a hold of me, then they should cast my vote in their favor. I had nothing but trust that my siblings would make the right decision

MARY

As the days began to turn into weeks, I became the unofficial greeter in the ICU. Our family and friends had commandeered a table that became "our" table for the time we were there. Other families had their areas too. Whenever they'd leave for a quick shower or to walk their dogs—whatever, I'd always throw a coat over a vacant chair to make sure their space was there when they returned. It's not that we didn't want anyone new to come in—that of course, is inevitable. I just understood what it meant to have your own space in the ICU waiting room. It offered some comfort and consistency in an otherwise very depressing and miserable place.

When you are in the ICU section of a hospital for more than a few days, you realize there are no secrets. Doctors come in to brief family members on their loved one's condition, on decisions that need to be made, or worse—to deliver the unthinkable news that the person you are there for has died. Everyone else in the waiting area can hear what the doctors are saying—except when they ask you to go into the private room off to the side. We all knew what that meant—and secretly hoped we wouldn't be the next family called in.

I got to know several of the families as each came in, full of fear, angst and worry. I did whatever I could to offer support, whether it was bringing Starbucks to someone who'd slept on the couch all night or sadly, attending the funeral of their loved one who passed.

JUNIOR

The pressure in the ICU is always underlined. The door of death is right there—all of the time. The pressure can build until suddenly the slightest thing can push an otherwise rational person over the edge. I'll never forget a young girl I met, who I called "Oreo Girl." The reason I called her Oreo Girl was because all she craved while she was waiting in the ICU was an Oreo cookie—not a mint

Oreo, which seemed to be the Oreo of choice in the waiting room—just a good old fashioned plain cream-filled Oreo. Her dad was in for a heart condition and a staph infection like our dad, so we bonded over the similarity in their cases.

"All I want is a real Oreo! Is that too much to ask?" she wailed before collapsing to the floor crying. The pressure had gotten to her in a way it hadn't seemed to penetrate our group. Perhaps we stood strong because we were never alone or because we knew that if we gave in to the pressure mounting against Dad, he might too. The only choice was to be strong and remain positive.

During our time in the ICU, we got to know several families whose loved ones lost their battles. They'd go into that room knowing what the doctors were there to say. They'd emerge a few minutes later, changed for life. One of the more interesting surprises was how often those people would return to the ICU the following day to shake hands, hug, cry on a familiar shoulder and thank everyone for their support. Sometimes they'd sit and talk for an hour trying to process their loss. Other times, it was just a way to connect with others who shared their pain for one final moment.

What I realized early on in this journey was that every family in that area was just like us. Some were only there for a few days but most of the families would be around for ten days or more. We had no idea at the time that we were looking down the barrel of a month or more of ICU hell.

MARY

We never talked about Dad dying. Not once. It was certainly the ten thousand-pound gorilla in the room, but my brothers and I never sat down and said, "This is what's going to happen with Dad dying." For the first couple of weeks, his condition was hour-by-hour. One hour he was doing great and the next, he wasn't. One hour his color looked pink and the next hour it was gray. When I first got to the hospital, someone came over and asked me if I wanted to meet with the chaplain. I was confused by their question because in that moment and for the days and weeks that followed, it never occurred to me that this might really be the end. At first I thought they were asking because they thought we were a religious family and might want to do some praying. What they were actually offering was a chance for the chaplain to deliver Dad's last rites. Thanks, but no thanks. I knew Dad was in dire straits—that he would have a tough road ahead of him—but I couldn't bear to think that he might actually die. Maybe I was in denial, but none of us thought that this was how Dad would ultimately go. Junior always joked that there would be some fantastic fireball or grand explosion involved when Dad's time came. All we could do was focus on the positive. I think we all got that trait from our dad—a trait I didn't really appreciate until this happened.

CHAPTER 4
Decision Time

I was kept in a semi-comatose state for the first couple of weeks in the ICU, while the doctors did their very best to make sure I was stable enough for the antibiotic treatments to work. The doctors knew I was in a tremendous amount of pain but there were also concerns about the infection. I was responding to the antibiotics but hadn't completely flushed the bacteria from my system. By February 13th, my blood cultures were negative of staph, which meant it was no longer in my bloodstream. My platelets and white cell count were also much better, but the sepsis was still present along my spine. I was consistently running a temperature, so Dr. Kevin Molk, my personal family doctor, met with an infectious diseases specialist, who thought my fever might have been caused by a pocket or pockets of abscess located around my knee or in my joints. Dr. Molk suggested doing a PET scan to determine the exact cause and location. A PET scan is a mobile, full-body scanner that travels from hospital to hospital and just happened to be at Sky Ridge that day. The full-body scan provides immediate results by using radiation to locate the abscesses. This way, doctors can see where they are and whether they can be drained. Unfortunately, after lots of dialogue, the doctors did not believe I was medically stable enough to be moved from my room, even if my bed and machines came with me. No matter how good an MRI is, it cannot show the detail that a PET scan can. Not being able to take advantage of the PET scan on that day was an unfortunate lost opportunity.

As an alternate solution, Dr. Molk ordered an MRI on my knee to look for swelling, as well as one on my back to check the progression of the infection along my spine. I'd undergone MRI's every few days since I arrived in the ICU, but the one they planned to do on this day would take several hours, which made it extremely intensive and taxing on my body.

When I finished with my MRI and was resting in my room, my doctors suggested that everyone go home to get some rest. Besides, it was Valentine's Day. Almost everyone there had a sweetheart they should've been with for the holiday. They'd all been there for two solid weeks and I am sure, needed a break. Even so, Gail and Mary didn't want to leave. They were sitting together in the ICU waiting room when they suddenly heard the words, "CODE BLUE, ROOM 20" over the loudspeaker.

Mary had sat in the ICU long enough to know the room numbers of every patient in the unit. Out of boredom one day, she went on the Internet and looked up the various codes and the meaning of the colors she heard called throughout the day so she could understand what each stood for. However this time, there was absolutely no confusion about what was going on—Room 20 was my room and *Code Blue* meant I was in cardiac arrest.

By chance, Dr. Barry Molk, the brother of my family doctor, who happens to be a cardiologist on staff at Sky Ridge, was in the ICU when they called the Code Blue. By the time he ran into my room, I had flatlined—that's hospital talk for "died." I had no heart-beat. He couldn't get one back so someone pulled all of the tubes out of my mouth and nose as Dr. Molk began performing CPR.

Ultimately, he was able to revive me and I started breathing on my own. Even though I couldn't talk, Dr. Molk spoke to me. He explained everything that happened. Apparently several of my tubes had become clogged with bile and mucus, which actually had the effect of suffocating me. My heart had stopped because of that and not because I was having a heart attack. My breathing was still labored though, because in addition to the cardiac arrest, I suffered respiratory arrest from a collapsed lung, which may have been caused by either the removal of the tubes from my mouth and nose or from the pressure of the chest compressions. I don't think we will ever know, but there were several minutes when I wasn't getting enough oxygen, which caused my heart to slow and then stop.

Dr. Molk told me he'd saved a lot of lives in the past, but I was the first who had his eyes wide open, as if I were awake throughout my resuscitation. I didn't remember a single moment of it and I couldn't talk because my throat was raw, but I sure was grateful that Dr. Molk was there.

GAIL

I immediately knew it was Dave's room when I heard the Code Blue. I wasn't exactly sure what that meant but I knew it was something bad. I wanted to rush over to be by his side but I couldn't get there before the doctor started working on him. After Dave was stabilized, Dr. Molk came down the hall to the waiting room to tell us he was all right. I was so relieved that I began to cry. This was the first time I'd let my emotions show since Dave was admitted to the hospital. It was a miracle that Dr. Molk was just steps away when Dave's breathing stopped. If it weren't for his fast actions, I'm not sure Dave would have survived.

From that day on, Dr. Barry Molk became one of my husband's greatest advocates throughout his illness. Even though he wasn't Dave's doctor before this happened, he became a good friend because of it. Dr. Molk stopped by Dave's room early in the mornings, sometimes arriving before I did on my way to the office. It was also Dr. Molk who sat our family down very early on and encouraged us to only say positive things to Dave when we saw him. Even if he was sleeping, he suggested we reinforce the positive by reassuring Dave that he looks good, stronger and better. He said there was great healing power in touch, so we should hold his hands, stroke his hair, rub his arms and legs and make any kind of physical connection he could feel, even if he was unconscious.

MARY

Chuck's girlfriend Bonnie shared an article she'd read about how people in comas can actually hear you. She said one of the most common things people talk about after coming out from a coma is the feeling of being alone. Once I read the article, and at Dr. Molk's suggestion, I completely changed how I spoke to my dad. I wasn't sure he could hear me, but every morning I walked into his room and gave him a pep talk like I was a coach getting ready to send my fighter into the ring.

"Good Morning, Dad! You're in the ICU at Sky Ridge. You're really sick but you are improving and I want you to know that right now Dave Jr. and John are out there and they are playing cards around the corner from your room. None of us are leaving until you come home with us. You are not alone, Dad. It's going to be ok."

My dad is not a touchy-feely kind of guy. He's always been more of a rough and tough John Wayne cowboy type than a Cary Grant. One of the only nice memories I have of being in the ICU with my dad is being able to hold his hand. If he were awake, he'd never let me do that. It's not that he isn't a kind man—he's the best. It's just he was never very affectionate. When I was growing up, instead of hugging me, Dad used to reach out to shake my hand. I always laughed and said, "Dad, just give me a hug!" It's not the kind of man he ever was. So in a strange way, I was grateful to be able to hold my father's hand and share a connection I longed for but never had.

After my cardiac arrest, I was still kept pretty drugged up and in a semi-conscious state. There were days I was out of it and completely non-responsive and other days when I was awake and able to have conversations I wouldn't remember moments later. Sometimes my talk sounded more like gibberish or a foreign language that only made sense to me. Other times, especially during the first four weeks in the ICU, even if I wanted to speak, I couldn't, so I'd do my best to communicate with my eyes.

When certain people, including Gail, Adam and Margaret, walked into the room, I'm told I would light up. My gaze would fixate on their faces and I'd never look away. I still couldn't move my arms or legs but I could move my eyes so I'd focus them and do my best to let my visitors know how I was feeling. Whenever Dr. Barry Molk came into my room, I'd open my eyes very wide, as if to say I felt good, safe and secure with him there. When the doctors and nurses were discussing something about my treatment I didn't agree with, I'd give a certain look that let Junior, Mary or anyone else who knew me well know that I wasn't going for it.

— DR. BARRY MOLK —

Dave's doctors were contemplating doing tracheoplasty on him right around the time he had his cardiac arrest. When I spoke to him about it, his eyes kept getting wider and wider and his breathing started getting harder and harder. He experienced all of the signs I'd expect to see from someone about to have a panic attack. He'd calm down for a minute, and then he'd widen his eyes again. I could tell his eyes were shouting, "NO!" He couldn't talk, but he was definitely communicating that he wasn't happy with what he was hearing, as tears welled up in his eyes.

After the results of my MRI came back, Dr. Prusmack explained that my situation had become dire. Although I had been responding to the antibiotics, the infection along my spine was still very invasive. The only way to save my life was to operate along my spinal cord and spinal nerve to remove the infection. It's a delicate procedure because he would have to scrape my spinal cord and nerves with a scalpel to remove the sacks of pus. There was no margin for error. He was somber as he described the horrific situation to my family and friends. He wouldn't promise anything positive, as he knew this would be a Herculean effort to save my life.

The anesthesiologist for the surgery was there too. He reiterated that although the surgery was risky, the medical instability of my failing organs made it even worse. They needed to drain the sacks of pus that had attached to my spine to relieve the pressure in my back, which was likely causing my paralysis. If they didn't, chances were, I'd be paralyzed for life. In all likelihood, they could eliminate some of the staph, but they would probably never get rid of all of it.

"What if you don't operate?" someone asked.

"He is going to die." Both doctors confirmed their worst fear.

Having just come through a heart scare, my family and friends huddled together as a group to make a decision about this latest news, since I was in no condition to do it myself—and they knew they had to make it fast.

JUNIOR

The only time we ever wavered in a decision as a group was when the doctors were contemplating putting a trachea tube in dad. We were worried about putting the tube in before dad's surgery. Some decisions in the ICU have to be made quickly on the fly, while others allow for a little time. This was one of those decisions. There was something telling each of us not to do the surgery now but we knew that scar tissue can form in the trachea that could cause permanent damage to his throat and ability to speak. We got them to hold off for a couple of days, but we knew it was down to the wire.

The doctors were planning to do my tracheotomy on February 15th, the day before they wanted to schedule my back surgery. I overheard a conversation between the nurses and doctors in my room about moving the time of that procedure from 5:00 PM to 1:00 PM. The doctor was suggesting they ought to do the procedure earlier that day because Dr. Prusmack was scheduled to do his operation the following day and they wanted to give me a slightly broader window to recover before going under the knife again with Prusmack. I hadn't uttered a word since the tubes had come out from my cardiac arrest. It's not that I didn't want to, I simply couldn't because they had reinserted the ventilator tube down my throat, which was now extremely raw, sore and very uncomfortable. As the dialogue continued in my presence, my daughter Mary turned toward me and noticed I was crying. That's when everyone was certain that I didn't want the tracheotomy. I knew it meant I would lose my voice. I could handle being paralyzed because I could learn to move in a different way, but the thought of losing my ability to communicate—one of my greatest assets in building my business and helping others achieve their dreams—was more than I could accept. I cherished my public speaking skills and couldn't fathom the idea of never being able to communicate, inspire and motivate an audience again. Now more than ever, I wanted to preserve my voice so I could use it to share this journey of survival, this journey of learning to be the best you can be with what you have left. Of course, I had a long road ahead of me, but somewhere not so deep inside of me that day, I inherently understood that my voice would be the platform with which to share this experience someday. I'm so glad the family held off making that decision, because it turns out that I didn't need the procedure after all.

JOHN

We quickly figured out that if you want to get a doctor to talk to you, don't sit in the waiting room because doctors don't come into the waiting room. They have four or five patients who each have families on pins and needles sitting there. If they came in, they would get questions from all sides. We noticed that they had a tendency to walk up the hallway to their office after leaving the ICU. We found that the best way to get their attention was to stand in that hallway because they had no choice but to walk by you. Dad was declining and Junior and I were in the hallway talking about what the next steps should be and what to tell people, when we spotted Dr. Molk coming out of Dad's room. We asked him how Dad was really doing. He told us that Dad was in critical condition and still had a long way to go before he would be out of the woods. He looked at Junior and me and said, "There is a lesson here—you can be doing everything right in your life, and just because of a little tiny bug that has gotten into your system, a few days later you're in ICU fighting for your life." He looked right at me and said, "The lesson is, don't wait too long to start living your life." I have probably thought about that conversation every day since then. It certainly made me take a look at my life and what I have and have not been doing with it.

Everyone involved in the decision about my surgery knew my life had been filled with great adventure and risk. I've been a jet pilot, I've gone scuba diving all over the planet, I've enjoyed skydiving, and I've even attempted to fly a helium balloon around the world. But I've never entertained the thought of dying while trying. I've lived most of my life believing I was invincible. I never once contemplated that I would be in this situation. I'd been in the hospital several times over the course of my life for pretty minor things, such as a dislocated shoulder, some broken ribs and knee injuries, but I was in and out in a couple of days.

This time, things were different. This was an unforeseen horizon, one that rose up quite unexpectedly and one that was very unwelcome.

After listening to the doctors, it was evident to everyone that my surgery was risky and that if I managed to survive it, there was a strong chance that I'd be paralyzed for the rest of my life. They debated about what I would want and quickly came to a unanimous decision.

They told the doctors to operate.

CHAPTER 5
Wanting to Die

About four weeks into my ordeal, I was still in excruciating pain. I hurt so badly and by this time, the medication I was on was having the added effect of making me feel depressed. I still had tubes down my throat, which I never found comfortable.

What's more, I had wires, lines and drips plugged into my body—all of which were attached to some type of apparatus that was keeping me alive. Dr. Barry Molk had come into the room to check on me as he had done so many other nights before. I lit up whenever he came for his daily visits. He'd hold my hand and talk to me, telling me that things were getting better. He'd pat my arm while encouraging me to fight and stay strong.

"Never give up, Dave." Dr. Molk's presence was always uplifting to my spirits. Sometimes he'd squeeze my hand and ask me to do the same. If I could, I did. If not, I'd always blink my eyes or nod my head to let him know that I could hear him.

On this particular night however, something was off. When Dr. Molk came into the room, I was blank. I didn't respond to him in any way.

While my memories of those first four weeks are pretty scarce, there is one moment I will never forget. Shortly after Dr. Molk left that night, I recall suddenly being unusually lucid—and believe me, there weren't many of those nights during those first few weeks. I'd come to the realization that I was going to die and

I had started an inner dialogue with myself about what that really meant. It was a very logical discussion—one I am certain wasn't a dream and one that didn't personify who I was or how I had lived my life.

—— **DR. BARRY MOLK** ——

For weeks, every night I left the hospital wondering if Dave would be alive when I came back the next day. As a cardiologist, I can see when a patient finally gives up. I watched Dave fight harder than anyone I have met in the ICU. But now there was a look that only people who are giving up get. His eyes were glazed over and dull. He had no response to anything I was asking him to do. I went home that night knowing Dave had given up and there was nothing I could do to help him.

You've lived a helluva life, I thought. *But living like this isn't worth it.* I wanted to sit up but I couldn't. I was still paralyzed and the pain never stopped—ever. My quality of life was diminishing, but from where I was sitting, it appeared to be gone altogether. I couldn't talk because of the tubes down my throat and even if I could, at the moment, I was immersed in my own personal pity party. I couldn't imagine living another day like this. No way. I was done putting up a fight. I needed rest, relief and was craving peace. The only way I could think of to get peace was to die.

I began thinking through all of the details that I might have overlooked, starting with my estate plan, my family's needs and of course, whether my company was properly prepared for my departure. As far as I could tell, everything had been put in its proper place. Gail would be cared for, my kids were living good independent lives and my company was already running as it should without me. Whether my friends and colleagues knew it, my contingency plan had been put into place long before I arrived at Sky Ridge—and though I wasn't completely aware of it at the time, it was working just as I had hoped. My management team excelled in my absence, operating the company every bit as well as I would have had I been there. In retrospect, I find that both satisfying, because I had an influence in their training and in getting them to that point, and yet very humbling, because it meant that I wasn't indispensable.

With that mental checklist complete, I began to think about all of the ways I might be able to die. I tried to slow down my breathing, which resulted in me fading in and out of consciousness. I held my breath, but that didn't stop my heart either. I thought, "Go ahead—die. Stop breathing and let your heart stop beating." But it wouldn't.

Several hours passed before I realized I must have fallen asleep. My first thought when I came out of my drug-induced fog was, "You coward! You're such a loser. For forty years of your life you have given speeches on never quitting!"

I had never quit *anything* in my life.

I've been in combat and airplane crashes.

I've driven NASCAR and survived dangerous category 5 rapids.

I've done every adventurous thing known to mankind, including feats that could kill you, and never once stopped myself out of fear that I wouldn't make it through.

There were so many people fighting to keep me alive, giving of themselves in unimaginable ways, and all I was thinking about now was giving up.

"That makes you the worst kind of hypocrite. If you give up now, you will wash away forty years of delivering speeches to tens of thousands of people, encouraging them to never give up, to deal with whatever obstacles have been put in their way, to find the courage to face those obstacles head on! Screw it. I won't quit. Not now, not ever!"

The minute I had that epiphany, I made up my mind to keep on fighting. I owed it to everyone to never give up. I've had a lifetime of minor and major setbacks just as I've had minor and major accomplishments. Each one taught me that this is not the end of the world. You move on. I learned courage from the soldiers I stood next to in the fields of Vietnam and from the way Gail handled her challenges knowing she would be partially paralyzed for the rest of her life. She never once cried, never complained and she never missed a therapy session. She never looked back and said a word about what she lost. Instead she looked forward toward her future and figured out a way to recover. Gail's quiet persistence was an inspiration to me and to so many others who watched her battle the odds. It certainly was a learning experience; one that taught me that even if you had your nose bloodied, you have to get up and keep on fighting.

So, I made up my mind right then and there that if I was going to be a paraplegic, I'd be the best damned paraplegic in the world. I'd learn to play wheelchair hockey or basketball, and to be just as tough as an able-bodied person. I wouldn't lose who I am just because I lost the use of my legs or arms. I knew I had the inner strength to do whatever it took. I would not spend the rest of my life bedridden. I just needed to rally my determination again.

Everyone has moments in his or her life that turn into weeks and sometimes months or even years. The most important thing to remember is that moments do pass. No matter how bad it hurts, the world does come back into focus. You have to live your life one step at a time. Perhaps you will take small steps instead of giant leaps, but as long as you keep moving forward, you will always be taking your next step.

I am a fairly smart man and though I don't profess to be nearly as smart as a lot of my colleagues, one thing I am sure of is that I can outwork anybody. I acquired that strong ethic and mental toughness at a young age while growing up on a farm in the Midwest. Every year from March through October, we raised white-faced heifers that grazed on the land of our pasture. When fall came, they went off to the butcher.

The heifers were constantly getting out of the pasture. One day, my father came home to find that a cow had gotten out. She was several hundred feet away, down near our pond. We needed to go get her and bring her back up to the barn. As we made our way toward the cow, I noticed my father was carrying a twenty-pound cinder block with a large linked chain attached to it that we sometimes used as a dog lead. When we reached the wayward heifer, I watched in horror as my father wrapped the chain around her head. He dropped the block on the ground and then told me to get a switch. He wanted me to hit the cow a couple of times to get her to move. We were trying to get her to budge, but she was being obstinate.

I was just a little fella at the time, so I could lie on the ground

under the legs of that old cow and hit her with the switch. I
wasn't hitting her very hard, but I assure you I was scared to
death she would stomp on me. When the cow still refused to
move, my father lost his temper. He grabbed me off the ground,
threw me up against the side of the cow and said, "Make up your
mind whether you are more afraid of me or the cow." I don't
recall my father ever getting mad like that before or after that day,
but I do remember I was no longer afraid of that cow. I beat her
like a drum, whacking away until she finally moved.

That moment stayed with me the rest of my life and frankly
helped put fear in its proper perspective. Many years later, I was in
a foxhole with some buddies in Vietnam when I began laughing
for no reason at all.

"What's so funny?" someone asked.

"I ain't afraid of that cow, I'll tell you that." They didn't
know what I meant, but I sure did.

I've thought about that day at my father's farm many times
over the past sixty years, and here I was, lying in my hospital bed
staring down the cow yet again.

Eleanor Roosevelt once said, "You gain strength, courage,
and confidence by every experience in which you really stop to
look fear in the face. You are able to say to yourself, 'I have lived
through this horror. I can take the next thing that comes along.' "

There have been many terrible times throughout the course
of my life. I was not an overnight success. I worked very hard
and made a lot of mistakes that I've had to pay for along the way.
There have been so many make-or-break moments in our company's history when I've stood back and wondered if I'd thrown
away twenty years of my life—times when I risked losing it all
because of those mistakes. When you look at anyone in life whose

actions appear heroic, you must realize that they actually got to that plateau step by step and more often than not, by taking very small steps. Through all the life events I've experienced—whether it was being in combat, building my business or suffering extraordinary financial difficulties during downward markets—I somehow perservered. I managed to live through each challenge, overcome it and ultimately learn that *what doesn't kill you makes you stronger*. In reality, those life experiences gave me the fortitude, the toughness, to face the hardest battle of my life—which was first and foremost to survive and then to learn to walk again, one step at a time.

CHAPTER 6
Baby Steps

Against all odds, my first surgery was a success. My blood sugar, blood pressure, heart rate and breathing were starting to progress well, and I was able to respond to touch and recognize voices. When I awoke, I felt no pain in my upper or lower back. Although it was a temporary reprieve, it was a much needed one.

Miraculously, the doctors were able to locate and drain the fluid buildup along my lower spinal column as planned. They rid me of as much of the staphylococcus bacteria as they could, but the test results indicated that the fluid they removed did not have as much of the infection in it as they expected. The next seventy-two hours would provide the doctors with enough information to help them decide what to do next.

Within a day or two of surgery, my ever-present fever had dissipated, which was a very good sign that the infection was losing ground. I began to stabilize for the first time in a month. One of the best moments for me was finding out that my ventilator tube would finally be removed. I was deliriously happy when I heard that news. The thought of being able to completely close my mouth was heavenly. I knew it would be uncomfortable for the next few days as I got used to breathing on my own again, but that was ok. I even looked forward to coughing up my own phlegm because that would be another small step toward my recovery. We all recognized that the process would be slow. In fact, someone in the group dubbed it my "Baby Steps" toward healing and recovery.

When I first awoke from my coma, I had the mind of a child. I'm told my cognitive reasoning was that of a four year old. (Well, that might have been true before my coma too, but only after a few drinks!)

I know I must have been really out of it because I'm not at all a touchy-feely kind of guy, but when I opened my eyes and my daughter, who was standing next to me, asked to hold my hand, I said, "Yes!" Of course, I also asked about Gail and how she was. I was more worried about her than myself.

With each and every day bringing me closer to moving on with my life, I had to consider what that life might actually look like. At the time, I didn't have the mental ability to really consider the options. I still had to learn the basics all over again, like how to eat, chew and swallow my food. Sitting up in bed was considered a great accomplishment—one I met as often as I could, but not often enough to satisfy me.

My throat remained raw and tender as I tried my best to start talking. I needed to give my voice and vocal cords a rest, so the doctors curtailed visits for a few days. I spent the next two weeks slowly doing some limited range-of-motion exercises on my left arm and leg. The right side of my body was still paralyzed.

I was finally able to have a shave on February 19th, and for the first time in weeks, began to resemble my old self. My nurse Jean gave me that first shave. I liked the results so much I asked her do it throughout the rest of my stay. Though she used an electric razor, I was still grateful for her steady hand. It's a strange experience to look into a mirror and not recognize the face staring back at you. Something as simple as shaving helped me reconnect to my old life, to my old self. It gave me a sense of familiarity that I found both comforting and inspiring.

My chest tube was removed about a week after my ventilator, which meant I could finally sleep more comfortably than I had in weeks. My breathing had become deliberate and steady, which was extremely encouraging. I was showing all sorts of signs of improvement, so these baby steps seemed to be paying off. I was eager to complement my range-of-motion work with physical therapy, but my doctors said I wasn't quite ready for that yet.

When I was able to spend more of my days awake and aware, my neurologist regularly stopped in to see me and was very pleased with my responses to his commands, including his requests for me to stretch my arms, move my hands and fingers and wiggle my toes. It appeared that the paralysis was temporary, but they wouldn't know for sure until the infection was totally under control. I would have a lot of hard work ahead of me to regain my strength and the use of my muscles, but he was encouraged that I could get there. I was more than willing to do whatever it took to make that happen.

When I first arrived at the hospital, I don't believe anyone thought I would be there for an extended period of time. Hell, as far as we were concerned, I went in for treatment of a chronic back ailment and within days I was fighting for my life. In the beginning, I think everyone believed they could keep this a family matter. But as the days turned into weeks, it was obvious that something had to be said, especially to the team at RE/MAX. As so often is the case when people don't have answers, crazy rumors began to fly about me. There was talk that I was in rehab, had run away with a secretary and was nowhere to be found, and that

I was dying from cancer. The wildest of these was that I'd been bitten by a shark!

Margaret Kelly was beginning to field inquiries about my absence from all over the country. Junior was getting emails, phone calls and text messages from family friends who couldn't reach me. Mary and Junior had both done an excellent job keeping everyone in our inner circle informed on a daily basis, but even those emails were written in a way that protected my privacy. There was never a single correspondence referencing the chance that I might not make it. Most of their notes were simple, to the point and generally more positive than they should have been. The kids realized that even though it was their father in the hospital fighting for his life, it was also the chairman and co-founder of a very large corporation. They knew the dynamics of the company had to be considered with each and every update they sent out. I was so unstable for the first several weeks that they really couldn't give a precise update anyway. As they described it, my condition was changing hour-by-hour and then day-by-day. What was true on Monday was not neccesarily true on Tuesday, and so on. This uncertainty was challenging for everyone and might have caused chaos in an already stressful circumstance. No good would have come from that, so they chose to be as open as they could, yet close to the vest with highly personal concerns.

At headquarters, no one outside of a very small group of top officers and the board of directors knew what was really happening early on. By mid-February though, Margaret shared my condition very openly and honestly with all of the officers, so they would know how serious my situation had become. She held off on making any further statements until we were certain about my prognosis.

MARGARET KELLY

Dave is the kind of man who wants to take care of everyone else when they are sick. He wants to be the hero. Now he had to be dependent on other people. For him, that was tough. But for the people who could actually go and do something for him, it was a way to pay him back.

I wasn't sure if he was going to make it. I had holy water from St. Peter's Basilica at the Vatican that I wanted to use to bless him so if he passed, he would go in peace. It was rare to get a moment alone with Dave when he was in the ICU. One of his kids always accompanied his visitors to his room. This time, I wanted a private moment alone. At this point, he wasn't my boss so much as a friend who needed way more than anyone there could give him. I spoke to John about my intentions, which he graciously honored. When I sat next to Dave, I used the water to make a cross on his forehead and I said a prayer. I knew there was someone who had the power to heal Dave and He wasn't wearing a white coat or stethoscope around His neck.

I reminded Dave that even in the rare moments when there was no one else in his room, he was never really alone because it was my belief that God was always with him. Dave and I have never really seen eye to eye on our religious beliefs. I prayed for Dave every day. I knew it would take a miracle for him to survive.

In addition to running our company in my absence, Margaret came to the hospital to visit as often as she could. Our relationship goes beyond chairman and CEO—we are really great friends. Margaret had been through her own personal health crisis a few years back and I was right there by her side every step of the way. I never let her feel alone during a single hospital stay, and now, even with a very full plate of her own, she was returning that same compassion. She sat by my bedside doing whatever she felt was right to keep me feeling as normal as I could, from clipping my fingernails, which the hospital wouldn't do, to combing my ever-growing partially blonde but quickly graying hair. I was beginning to resemble Howard Hughes in his really reclusive years. I hadn't appeared this much like a hippie since the early days of founding RE/MAX and even then, it wasn't my best look. Margaret is a much more religious person than I am and was curious about my near-death experience when I flatlined. She kept asking me if I saw any bright lights or long tunnels. I told her I didn't see anything like that.

"Well, was there anything dark in the distance?" she asked with her usual wit and humor. I didn't respond for fear my answer might incriminate me.

Even though the real estate press had picked up on my illness pretty early on, they were polite enough to never publicly say a word. They knew what was happening, but had the decency and respect for Gail, my family and me to allow us to have our privacy. Some members of the real estate press are my close friends, so they came by to see me without ever allowing anything to be printed in one of their publications.

The local newspapers and television stations looked the other way too. Someone approached Junior in the hospital and asked him how I was doing. Uncertain how he should answer, he simply responded, "On the record or off?"

"Junior, we've kept your daddy off the record the whole time. I am genuinely concerned, so that's why I'm asking."

"To be honest, it's touch and go. We don't know what's going to happen." Junior spoke the truth with the hope that it would sway the reporter to let it go.

"We think the world of your father, so you tell us what to do and we'll do it." In a world where tabloid media is so prevalent, it was a breath of fresh air to find a community of journalists with so much editorial integrity. I will never be able to express my appreciation for their decency and their respect of my privacy, as well as for giving me the opportunity to heal without being under their microscope.

Throughout my stay in the ICU, there were horrible moments of humiliation and lack of dignity no one wanted to make public, especially the loss of my ability to go to the bathroom on my own. I didn't have the mobility or strength to use a bedpan, so my hospital bed became my toilet. When I was conscious enough to tell someone I had to go to the bathroom, they would roll me on one side and build a makeshift commode out of plastic bags that fit around my rear end. When I was done, they'd wash and clean me. I assure you this was not a pleasant experience for anyone, especially the technician who was assigned to me at that particular moment. From my perspective, it was embarrassing as hell. But what choice did I have? It was what it was. Even if the humiliation was slightly dulled at times by the pain medication, I will never forget the experience of praying that I wouldn't crap the bed.

The nurses and technicians were always kind and never made things more uncomfortable for me than they already were. They'd lay a pillowcase across my groin and act like they didn't notice all of my body parts hanging out as they gave me bed baths. I played dumb, often pretending I wasn't *really* naked. But of course, I was.

MARY

I stopped in to see Dad and asked him if he wanted me to stay for a bit. I promised I wouldn't talk! He was able to nod his head, "no."

I didn't take it personally. In fact, it was progress.

Before I left, he began talking to me about his arm. I asked if he was in any pain? Again, he nodded, "no," and then lifted his left arm from his hand to his elbow up on his own. He raised it again, and this time, moved his left leg as well. Though he still couldn't move the upper part of his arm to his shoulders or his right arm or leg, this was tremendous progress.

"You see, Dad? The doctors were right! They said you'd be able to move your arms again—you just needed time."

Dad nodded his head, "yes," before dozing off to sleep.

It was amazing to see the pride in his face and the joy in his eyes because he could move of his own volition.

ADAM CONTOS

Although Dave was showing small signs of improvement almost daily, the infection was still inside his body. It wasn't clear yet if another surgery would be required to remove the remaining sepsis, but based on the amount of pain Dave was still in and the length of time the infection had now been in his system, the probability was high that they would need to go in a second time. The infectious disease doctor said the best-case scenario would be twelve weeks of antibiotic therapy from the date of his first surgery, February 16th through the middle of May. He would have to continue the antibiotics for months to come, if not longer.

Dr. Molk's main focus was on getting Dave to start moving his body so it did not deteriorate any more than it already had. The biggest threat at this point was developing bedsores from being immobile. If that were to happen, Dave would likely have a harder time fighting off the infection. Even though his nurses were rolling him over every couple of hours, a bedsore had started to appear on his lower back. Although the doctors could clean and dress it, they couldn't do much more to keep it from getting worse until Dave was more stable. His best prevention would be getting strong enough to move and eventually getting up on his own. The sooner Dave could move, the better.

By February 22nd, I was showing improvements in every area, including my kidneys and limited mobility. I was able to move my left leg and lift my left arm off the bed, bending at the elbow. My progress may have felt slow, but given the fact that my body had been in shock from the virus and I had been in the ICU for nearly a month, it was actually quite a spectacular improvement over what they originally predicted. I wasn't out of the woods by any means, but I was certainly taking the necessary steps along the right path. It had been only a week since my surgery, but the doctors were actually talking to my family about moving me—in time—from the ICU into a long-term rehabilitation facility such as Craig Hospital, the same place where Gail had recovered from her accident twenty-nine years earlier.

Before I got sick I never gave much thought to the meaning of happiness or freedom. I was certainly an upbeat guy—and appreciative for all of my blessings. Every day since Vietnam had been a gift. I have always valued life and fought for freedom. I never took it for granted because I understood how quickly things can change. My life experiences brought me to this place of acceptance without questioning the reasons why. I am a very pragmatic individual, someone who chooses not to lose sleep over the inevitable challenges that come our way. My philosophy has always been to approach challenges head on. What's done is done. There's nothing you can do about it now except deal with the situation by accepting your circumstances.

George Bernard Shaw once said, "*Life is not about finding yourself. Life is about creating yourself.*" I created every corner of the life I was living before I got sick, and now I was faced with the notion of recreating myself in a new light—one which I never gave an ounce of energy to until now. I can't deny that there were many nights during my hospital stay when I lay awake wondering what I was going to do with the rest of my life because for the first time ever, I felt helpless, vulnerable and worst of all, dependent. My mind was impaired, my body still weak and unable to move, and my ability to reason through potential solutions was limited at best. It was frustrating and I was becoming discouraged by my feelings of despair.

By February 27th, my kidneys had recovered well enough for me to be taken off dialysis. I was very happy to get that news, as it freed up even more time in my day to focus on getting stronger and improving my movement. I spent the better part of that afternoon watching the Daytona 500. Having owned my own NASCAR team, there was a connection to the event that kept me extremely lucid throughout the day. I was still having challenges talking, but there was no doubt that I enjoyed watching the event with Junior, who shares my passion for racing.

Although I seemed to be slowly improving, my doctors were still quite concerned about the infection, so one of my infectious disease doctors ordered two MRI's. The first would look closely at the top of my neck and the second at my lower back to check on the healing of my spine and the effects of my limited movement. Each MRI would take two hours to complete, but it would give my doctors an accurate picture of where I was at.

After seeing the results of the MRI's, Dr. Prusmack explained that there was still a fair amount of pus in the lower region of my spine that he wanted to drain. Doing this would take additional pressure off of that area. In addition, the abscess in my neck had become smaller but it also appeared to create some excess scar tissue. Operating would allow Dr. Prusmack to clean up the scar tissue and provide more room in the neck area of my spine. He thought the excess scar tissue might be the reason I couldn't move my arms above my elbows, and although this surgery would be as delicate, if not more complicated, than the first, it was worth a try.

Dr. Prusmack and Dr. Barry Molk warned Junior that the surgery was risky. Since my health was still quite compromised and I had begun to run a fever again, there was a good chance that I wouldn't make it through. And if I did, there was an even greater probability that I would be paralyzed for life. Unable to make the decision for myself, my family and friends weighed the pros and cons together just as they did for the first surgery.

As Junior was listening to the doctors' opinion, Rudy Zupetz, the golf pro from Sanctuary, happened to come by for a visit. It was still early. Junior was lying on the sofa in my room.

"Hey, I brought you some orange juice," Rudy said to Junior. After hearing about the severity of the situation, Junior looked over at Rudy and said, "What do you think, Rudy?" Of course, he was just yanking his chain.

"I have to go!" Rudy said, as he quickly turned and walked out of the room. He wanted nothing to do with making that kind of decision. Who could blame him?

Naturally, Junior reached out to Gail, his brothers and his sister before agreeing to let the doctors do the procedure. They had a very sophisticated and mature understanding of what was going on and kept it that way.

On the evening of March 7th, Dr. Prusmack opened me up for the second time. Mary, Junior and Dr. Barry Molk were there to support me. They've told me it was a very scary time for all of them, but they were equally excited because if I came through the surgery without a hitch, it meant I was making progress. Somewhere deep in their hearts, if this surgery went well, then perhaps, magically or by design, I would be cured. They sat in the ICU waiting room sweating bullets for two very long hours.

Gail, Margaret and Adam were at the annual RE/MAX R4 convention in Las Vegas, so they were kept apprised of my condition through emails and phone calls. Since I couldn't be there to give the opening speech, Gail gave it in my absence. Believe me, I would have much rather been in Las Vegas than in an operating room that day.

Since Dr. Molk was on staff at Sky Ridge, he had access to all areas of the hospital. He was able to monitor the surgery throughout my time on the table. When the doctors finished, he broke the good news to the gang that I had come through the procedure and was comfortably resting in my room.

He said that a significant amount of the infection had been removed from the upper part of my neck. My doctors hoped this was the source of the paralysis on the right side of my upper body, but couldn't be sure until a little more time had passed.

My lower back showed good progress from the previous surgery, which meant the antibiotics were working. I am sure this news came as a huge relief for everyone there, as they had been sitting on pins and needles, waiting for hours.

Shortly before my second back surgery, Margaret and Gail sat down with the family and explained that we needed to tell the whole company *something*. They didn't want the false rumors to grow even larger. It just wasn't fair to anyone to allow suspicions to incubate. I was still too out of it to speak on my own behalf, so they decided that Margaret should make a brief statement to our membership. The statement was to be neither promising nor alarming. They didn't want to scare anyone because there was the possibility that I would bounce back, but they also didn't want to make it seem like everything was all right when I was struggling daily to stay alive. My condition was constantly changing. Just when the doctors thought they had one problem under control, another popped up. But the time for the talk had come.

Margaret called a meeting with the three hundred or so people who work at RE/MAX corporate headquarters in Denver to tell them what was going on without going into all of the gory details. She explained that I had some complications from a serious back condition and was in the hospital recuperating from surgery. The news was hard to hear, but no one said a negative word. I got nothing but unconditional love and support.

When visitors arrived, my kids did an excellent job of greeting them. They made everyone feel welcome and appreciated, and yet also shielded me from being seen in such a vulnerable state. I really was a gruesome sight, and a shell of the man the good people of RE/MAX had come to know over the years. My family didn't want a visitor's last memory of me to be a decrepit, decaying man in a hospital bed. They wanted my friends and colleagues to think of me strong, healthy and fierce, like a lion. Even though I didn't get to visit with so many of those who stopped by, I will never forget their desire to be there or their unwavering kindness and support for both my family and me.

I spent the next couple of weeks on heavy-duty antibiotics and slowly began to stabilize. I was still considered critical, but not nearly as critical as I had been in the weeks leading up to the second surgery. Being kept on the critical list had its advantages, though. The biggest one was that I could still receive around-the-clock care. If my condition had been downgraded, I wouldn't have had the same kind of monitoring.

Dr. Barry Molk continued to come by daily, encouraging me to fight the good fight.

"You've got a lot of staph left in you, Dave, which means you've got a long road ahead and I need you to be strong. Can you continue to fight for me?" He'd ask this in a very inspiring way that always made me want to say, "Yes."

A few weeks later, Dr. Molk came by my room around 11:00 at night. He and I had a very good exchange that resulted in me laughing for the first time in months. He left my room feeling "cautiously optimistic" about my recovery—the first real positive sign my family was given that I might actually beat this thing.

While I was recuperating, Junior showed me a bit of the opening session from the RE/MAX convention that had been uploaded to Facebook. I did my best to watch and understand why I couldn't be there, but it became a bit confusing for me. For a moment, I thought I was at a hospital in Las Vegas and could easily be taken to the convention in my hospital bed. I was clearly disconnected from my reality, but remember being so proud of Gail for staying strong and carrying on without me.

Throughout this experience, I worried about Gail more than myself. Night after night, she went home alone. She ate her dinner by herself, slept in an empty bed and did her best to keep a stiff upper lip. Even though I was still alive, from my perspective she was living the life of a widow, something I never considered before this happened. She inspired me every day in her own recovery, perseverance and determination, and she continued to inspire me now more than ever. For the first time in my life, I understood what it was really like to stand in her place—to face a life that wasn't the one we had planned with a willingness to adapt as a means to survive.

FROM THE DESK OF MARGARET KELLY

2/27/12

Hello everyone,

I'd like to take a moment to share some news about Dave Liniger.

Here's what's happened over the past few weeks. Dave was feeling severe back pain, so he went to the hospital to get it checked. Doctors confirmed a problem in his back and also found a widerspread infection, which needed to be addressed before anything else was done.

By last week, things had improved, and Dave received the go-ahead for back surgery to relieve the pain and pressure causing him trouble. Everything went well; his doctors called it a textbook surgery. Although Dave is still in the hospital and has a lot of healing to do, he's making progress and feeling better.

Until recently, Dave was hopeful about attending R4. He really wanted to be there, but for now he needs to rest, avoid travel and follow doctor's orders, which is no easy task for him.

We don't want to overwhelm the Linigers, so please, no cards, calls, emails or flowers; Dave and Gail know how much you care about them and can feel your thoughts and support. If you want to reach out, we've created a virtual get-well card on Facebook, where you can express yourself and share a personal message.

R4 is going to be a fantastic event, as strong as ever. Dave expects to hear some great stories from Las Vegas, and we won't let him down.

I'm looking forward to seeing many of you at R4 next week.

Sincerely,

Margaret Kelly

Margaret Kelly
Chief Executive Officer
RE/MAX World Headquarters

BRUCE BENHAM

I am a positive man by nature but my positivity about Dave's situation was shattered a lot because of the fluctuation in his condition. I kept hearing about how critical he was and all of the other variables that kept him from getting better faster, which made me scared yet hopeful at the same time. Dr. Prusmack has also been my doctor over the years, so I felt comfortable enough asking him questions about Dave's illness and prognosis. He told me that Dave was in very serious condition, but it looked as if there was a good chance he'd stabilize. I didn't know anything about staph infections before Dave got sick. I had no idea how damaging they could be to the human body. Dr. Prusmack told me he was especially worried that Dave might have severe nerve damage from the staph infection. If your nerves are damaged, they're healable, but they heal a lot slower. So what might cause an injury in minutes can sometimes take months or even years to heal. Dr. Prusmack explained that nerves get angry quickly and they forgive very slowly. I never expected Dave's staph infection to be so vicious, let alone impact everything else from his kidneys to his lungs. What I did know was that it would take a miracle for Dave to pull through this, and if he were given that chance, it would take time—lots of time.

JOHN

I was in the hospital every day with Dad for the first month. When he had turned the corner and we could start making plans for rehab, I started slowing down—mainly because I was becoming stressed. I am physically strong, but because of the blood-thinning medication I take, it is easy for me to get sick. Sure enough, I started getting ill, which gave me a chance to step out. I let the rest of the family take over. I have the same type-A personality as my dad—it's the thing that made me such a good pilot. But taking control and making decisions from this point forward was the exact wrong thing to do in this situation. I have a strong mind and I know there are times when I should bow out. I was glad I was there at the critical moments though, and would be there whenever I could going forward.

CHAPTER 7

35 Days of Hell

On March 14, 2012, just eight days after my second surgery, I was stable enough to move from the ICU at Sky Ridge to Craig Hospital, where I would continue my very long and challenging road of healing. I was very ready to get out of the ICU and move forward with my next step toward recovery. My insurance company however, had other plans. They didn't approve my move to a rehabilitation facility specializing in spinal cord and head trauma injuries because I had neither. It was a tedious battle to finally get my transfer approved, but once we did, I was taken by ambulance, accompanied by Junior while Mary and her husband Jeff followed behind.

By the time I arrived at Craig, I was slowly becoming my old self again in spirit. Of course, my body had a long way to go before it could catch up to where it was. I had lost so much muscle from being in bed for such a long time that I was literally skin and bones. My children gave me leg massages to help get my circulation flowing, but there was nothing there. They said it felt like they could touch the bones right through my paper-thin layer of skin. If I had any hope of rebuilding muscle, I needed to get out of bed and start moving.

On one of my first days at Craig Hospital, a doctor came into my room to tell me the story of Sir Ernest Shackleton. As soon as the name fell from his mouth, Junior and Mary burst out laughing. You see, I've been a fan of the great explorer Shackleton for many years. My kids all grew up hearing me tell the story of his heroic Antarctic expeditions, especially what became known as the Imperial Antarctic Expedition from 1914-1917. Shackleton was attempting to cross the continent from sea to sea. His ship, called the *Endurance*, became trapped in pack ice and was crushed before rescuers could reach him and his team. Shackleton set out to get help and returned two years later to save his crew members, who all survived. As a result of his valiant efforts, he became known for his leadership abilities under the most extreme circumstances.

The doctor stood in my room and said, "Dave, we're looking at running a marathon together, and today is the first step toward our first mile."

Of course, I was still paralyzed, so I would need to learn how to walk again before I could enter the race, so to speak. But that wasn't the real obstacle standing in my way. There was something else that needed to be dealt with before I could even consider beginning my rehabilitation and physical therapy.

The next part of my story isn't for the squeamish, so if you are the kind of person who gets queasy at the thought of blood, you may want to skip the next few pages. Remember, you've been warned!

As a result of being in my hospital bed so long, mostly in a highly drugged state and unable to move, I developed what I now refer to as a *world class butt sore*. My sore didn't start on the outside and work its way inside; essentially, it began as an interior wound that burrowed its way through to my outer skin, revealing a tunnel to my tailbone and connective tissue. It started from the staph infection within my body and literally ate away layers of my muscle and skin until it created a giant hole in my back that a fully-grown man could put his fist through. Despite the nurses' best efforts to turn me every couple of hours, this very large bedsore just above the crack of my derrière had become increasingly infected. Bedsores are injuries to skin and underlying tissues that result from prolonged pressure on one spot. They usually develop in areas on skin that cover bony parts of the body, such as the heel, ankles, hips or buttocks.

Let's be clear about something. I am a fiercely competitive man. I like to win, and if you happen to beat me, you can bet that I put up a damn good fight. This was one contest, however, I'd rather have been left out of!

The doctors discovered my bedsore while I was at Sky Ridge, but my condition had been so severe, it was actually the least of their worries until they could get my staph infection and other ailments under control. By the time I arrived at Craig Hospital to start my rehabilitation, my bedsore had become one of the worst they'd ever seen. There was no hope that it would heal on its own. A bedsore that makes it to this serious stage often causes extensive destruction, including tissue death, and damage to muscle, bone and supporting structures such as tendons, joints, and the body capsule. The doctors would have to perform flap surgery, which required cutting the skin above my tailbone into three pizza slices, and then pulling them over the open wound to close the gap in my back.

At first, I didn't want anyone to see the sore. It was nasty-looking and not something one rushes to show off. Nevertheless, doctors and nurses from all over the hospital were stopping by my room to get a peek at my...uh...cheeks because mine was such a severe case. After a while, it got to the point where any time someone stopped by my room, I'd greet them with a hearty, "Hey, want to see my butt sore?"

The doctor who performed the surgery was a well-known plastic surgeon. His technique for closing the wound involved intertwining muscles and blood vessels before draping the skin and securing it with stitches. While the surgery was complicated, the recovery would be the worst phase. For the sutures to take and allow the skin to heal, I had to be bedridden again, unable to move even an inch for thirty-five days. The doctors told me that research indicated a much higher failure rate at four weeks than five, so the plan was to keep me still for five full weeks—which took me into the middle of May.

I'd already spent almost seven weeks lying still in a hospital bed at Sky Ridge, and several more weeks at Craig getting ready for my three to four month stay there. I had been fitted for physical therapy equipment and had set up my exercise and physical therapy programs before preparing for this—my third major surgery in two months. Again, they gave me medication for the pain, but this time around, I wasn't kept in a semi-comatose state for the recovery. As a result, I was painfully aware of every moment of time as it slowly ticked away.

Since the skin they used to cover the hole was extremely thin from pulling it tight, I had to be particularly careful not to bruise, scratch or overstretch my body or I'd risk reopening the wound and the healing process would have to start all over again.

When the surgeon finished the procedure, he was convinced that this was some of the very best work he'd ever done. The nurses came to check my sutures every two hours and invariably they'd say, "Time to roll over and look at your butt, Dave."

It got to the point where all I could do was find humor in the situation, so I'd always respond with a boastful, "Isn't that the prettiest ass you've ever seen?"

"No doubt about it," they'd say.

Before all of this happened, I had buns of steel—not squishy ones like they are now. But I did whatever I could to make the best of it all.

Other doctors from the hospital and even medical students came by to see me. When they arrived, I'd just laugh and tell them there was a tip jar in the corner. Looks weren't free. Once a businessman, always a businessman, right?

Wrong!

When nobody put money in the jar, I tried one last attempt to make everyone laugh.

"I'll show you mine if you show me yours." That didn't get me very far either.

Although I was making light of my situation, I was extremely lucky that the surgery was a success. The majority of paraplegics and quadriplegics who die each year die from these very types of sores. When you are paralyzed from the neck or anywhere below, you have no sensation in your body, so you can't feel the pain from developing sores. Often these patients don't even know they have sores unless somebody is looking for them. When you don't have a nurse to turn you every couple of hours, it can and often does become a life-threatening condition.

FROM THE DESK OF MARGARET KELLY

3/30/12

I'd like to update you again on Dave Liniger's health.

As most of you know, Dave checked into the hospital about eight weeks ago with severe back pain. Doctors determined that his discomfort was due to pressure built up through a severe staph infection.

He has since had two successful back surgeries to reduce the pressure and provide relief from the pain. The first occurred in February and the second in March, during R4. Both went very well.

Dave is still in the hospital and will be on antibiotics for another month or more, which is normal for a staph infection. He has also begun physical therapy, and it will take months for him to regain his strength. He's receiving the best care possible and his doctors are pleased with his progress.

Dave and Gail feel your love and support. We don't want to overwhelm Gail and the family while they are focused on Dave's recovery – so please, no cards, flowers, emails or calls. A virtual get-well card is still on Facebook; you're more than welcome to add your thoughts there.

Warm regards,

Margaret

Margaret Kelly
Chief Executive Officer
RE/MAX World Headquarters

LORIEL FIGIEL

I was one of Dave's day nurses at Craig Hospital. By the time he got to us in March, he'd had quite a long journey.

Not long after he got settled in, Dave began asking all of the right questions.

"What the hell's been going on for the past two months? Where am I? What happened?" I called that D-day because that was the day the doctor, all of his therapists and the techs were together with Dave's family in his room for the first time, telling him the story of where he'd been before, where he was at now, and what we were looking forward to doing, with the hope that he'd retain at least some of what we were saying. Dave was still very sick at this point, so we couldn't start the intake process a patient at Craig usually undergoes—a process that involves us, first and foremost, getting the patient out of bed and moving. Up until D-day, we had been speaking to Dave, but he wasn't with it enough to keep up with what we were saying. On this particular day, however, Dave awoke and for the first time since he arrived at Craig, was cognitively aware of what was going on around him.

When we told him about the thirty-five days of bed rest, I was worried that he might become confused and maybe try to get out of bed, bend his legs or do something that would jeopardize his recovery from the flap surgery. As it turned out, even in his most confused, upset, terrified moments, he was still the nicest patient I've ever taken care of. Granted, I worked with Dave in the daytime, and the nights were when his terror frequently set in. He tried to break free a couple of times, but someone would always talk him off the ledge and help him to understand the damage he could do if he didn't calm down.

Thirty-five days of bed rest doesn't do anybody any good mentally or emotionally. A lot of our patients struggle with it. We try to give them something more to do than stare at the ceiling. There's not a lot of therapy that can happen during that time, so the days have a tendency to run together. Sometimes the day and evening schedule gets flipped, so a patient might sleep all day and then be awake at night. Dave wanted to be on a regular and regimented schedule—one that felt familiar to him. Morning would come and he'd be ready to go for the day. Even though he was flat on his back, he'd always greet me with a hearty hello and the same questions:

"What's my schedule today? What are we doing?"

He looked forward to the therapy session or OT work he did on his arms like he was closing a large business transaction every single day. Dave came into this period with the best attitude, which made a world of difference in his results.

JOHN

I had the idea to put a page-a-day countdown calendar on the wall of Dad's room as a way of ticking down the time he had left in his thirty-five days of bed rest. We started with 35 and counted down. I thought it would help him pass the time and would serve as a reminder of what day he was on. I also rented every bad Western and Adventure movie I could find at Blockbuster. Dad seemed to enjoy "Man on a Ledge" and "Monte Walsh," a film starring Tom Selleck. I even got him into watching the Colorado Rockies games with me, but they were losing every night, so it got downright depressing for both of us. Because Dad has never been a big television watcher, we tried getting a special stand for his iPad so he could read while lying down, but that didn't work either. What really got Dad through this period were his friends and family visiting all the time. When we realized this was giving Dad the support he needed to get through the long stretch of bed rest, we opened the doors to everyone who wanted to come for a visit.

Admittedly, those thirty-five days were tough, but I got through them without breaking. There were moments when I wanted to scratch my feet, but mentally I had given in to doing whatever had to be done. I tried my absolute best to be the happiest person I could be toward the nurses, doctors, therapists and technicians. It wasn't easy, but the effort alone made a huge difference in my overall disposition. Given where I had been the past several months, I wasn't going to complain. Instead, I used the time in the most productive ways I could think of. I had Mary write my schedule out on a white dry-erase board every day so I could see it, change, or adjust it if I wanted to. I resolved pretty early on that I was going to be the best patient Craig had ever treated. I had always had a lot of stamina and never worried about doing the hard work in life. As I lay in bed, I likened my recovery to two of the greatest lessons I learned very early in my life after reading the book *Think and Grow Rich* by Napoleon Hill. I was an impressionable sixteen-year-old kid who didn't want to spend the rest of his life milking cows on our farm in Indiana. That book, which I've read more than forty times, has been a tremendous inspiration and influence in everything I have accomplished in business and in life. If you haven't read it, I strongly encourage you to. And if you have, go back and read it again, because its lessons have held up over time and are as relevant today as they were when the book was first published in 1937. Fifty years after reading that book forty years of having actively exercised its principles, and thirty years of teaching from it brought me to two very simple lessons that have ruled my world. The first lesson is simple: *Whatever the mind can conceive and believe, it can achieve.* The second lesson is to *write down any goal that is worth achieving, make it an obsession and convince your brain that you* can *accomplish it. Be sure that the goal is realistic, then decide what your step-by-step plan will be to achieve it.*

The lessons are really about being persistent, setting realistic goals and finding the right people to encourage you to attain them. As you start working toward your goal, you may have to stop, recalibrate, make adjustments and then get back to working toward that goal. But NEVER, ever give up until you reach it. My first goal while at Craig was to get past those thirty-five days. My friends and family would be my support system to get me through, and my doctors and nurses would make sure I didn't screw it up.

My second goal was to tell everyone at the hospital that I would be going home by June 29th—and that I would be *walking* out of there on that day.

The key thing to remember here is that I set my goals high, but I didn't set them out of reach. There *was* a possibility I could walk again. Bear in mind that what is achievable for one person may not be for someone else. When you're in a rehabilitation hospital with a spinal cord or brain injury, for instance, there are realistic goals and then there are those that can never be achieved. Even though great strides have been made in medical research, when a spinal cord is severed, it's still impossible to put it back together. A person with that kind of injury may have the goal to move a single toe, but that's not likely to happen. *Positive* thinking is healthy, but *possible* thinking matters too. The staff at Craig does their best to teach each patient about realism and hope, but if your goal is not possible, they will show you how to make the best of the options you have left. Positive thinking won't change the truth, but a positive attitude can help you get through the period of disbelief, grief and anger anyone would feel in such circumstances, so you can put together a plan for how to live your best life. That's what I tried to do every day by verbally making declarations about my intentions and refusing to give up. I made my goals my obsession.

During that time, I was permitted to do work only on my upper body; I couldn't even flex my head or neck. I had to remain flat and still. But I figured that if I had to be flat on my back, then I would at least strengthen my hands by squeezing a rubber ball. I asked one of the kids to get me a can of racquetballs that I could scrunch, and that's exactly what I did.

I couldn't stand yet, but I could practice wiggling my toes and stretching them several times a day until my range of motion got better and better.

As a way of helping me reach my big-picture goals, my family set smaller ones I could hit along the way. In addition to my countdown calendar, they taped other goals up on the wall of my room too. They were very creative and clever about it. For example, Mary brought in a picture of Peyton Manning throwing a football with one hand and pointing with his other. She added a caption bubble that read, "Look, it's Dave without his catheter!" They did everything they could to keep the atmosphere light and positive.

My attitude was simple. In order to get to the work I really wanted to do, I had to get through these thirty-five days of hell. I knew I would never be able to learn to walk if I didn't heal the hole in my backside first. I accepted the fact that I was going to be on bed rest for those five weeks and dealt with it by motivating myself to get to the other side. The mind is a very powerful tool that can work for or against you. This battle was every bit as mental as it was physical. I couldn't let the darkness that came at night control the outcome of my days. I had to be fearless, fight through the pain, and face the unknown.

"We must embrace pain and burn it as fuel for our journey."

-Kenji Miyazawa

During those days, I was fortunate to have so many friends stop by to help me pass the time. A buddy from the Marines, who lives more than a hundred miles from Denver, came to visit me almost daily. Dave Fisher, a friend who is a police officer, brought me a galvanized steel bucket.

"This is for your bucket list," he said. "You have to start thinking about things you want to do before you die."

Inside, there was a message that read, "This is from your kids. Let's go to Hawaii on vacation, and please take Officer Fisher with you!"

I thought that was very funny. What I realized, though, was that I had no bucket list. I've already done most of the things I've wanted to do in my life. Every day people get up and read another National Geographic and say, "I would like to go do that," but up until my hospital odyssey, I had the ability to go and do wherever I wanted, and I often did just that. I suppose learning to fly could be added to the list, but since I already have my pilot's license, it would have to be learning to fly like Superman.

I recall having read a book many years ago called *The Three Boxes of Life*. The book suggests that there are three boxes we all live in throughout our lives. The first box refers to your *learning years*, which include birth through your college education. The second refers to your *earning years*, which include college through retirement, and the third is playfully classified as your *yearning years*. These are the years that are supposed to be dedicated to your golden retirement, but because you can't physically do any of the stuff you could do when you lived in your other two boxes, you spend them yearning for what you could have or should have done before. The philosophy of the book is that one should live in all three boxes at the same time. It doesn't make sense to live in the earning years and save so much that you never take vacations or enjoy life by doing the things you love to do. I'll admit that when I was healthy, I was considered by many to be a workaholic. I was always the first one at the office in the morning, usually arriving by 5:00 AM. Even so, I always remembered to take time off. I never had a problem going on safari to Africa for four weeks at a time without calling home or checking in at work. I spent plenty of my weekends in Scottsdale or Lake Powell boating, fishing, golfing or spending leisurely time with my family. So as I reflected on my life, I knew I wouldn't be one of those guys who spent his golden years yearning. Not even during my prolonged hospital stay, when my future was uncertain. I was alive, which meant I would continue to live as I always had—with renegade gusto.

Anything I want to do, I know I can achieve. I may never run a marathon, but even when I was able-bodied, that wasn't one of the things on my long-term wish list anyway. The love of my life has been my business and my business accomplishments. I have done the adventure thing to no end, and truth be told, will continue to pursue adventure in the future. I love going over to a local racetrack on a Saturday night and pushing the younger drivers around. I get great pleasure from driving fast cars, flying airplanes, hunting, fishing and camping. And I can still do all of these things—maybe not to the extent that I once did, but I can choose to participate instead of spending the rest of my days watching from the sidelines. Where's the fun in that?

CHAPTER 8
White Rabbit

Since very early in my illness, about ten days into my stay at Sky Ridge, something very strange and terrifying had been happening. I was suffering panic attacks and vivid hallucinations. These occurred well into my time at Craig. Nothing in my life had ever given me anxiety before, nor had I ever suffered from claustrophobia. As a seasoned deep-sea diver, I've explored caves under water and never once felt symptoms like the closed-in feelings I was having in my hospital bed. Everything about my situation was making me uncomfortable and filled with angst, from the tubes in my mouth to the heaviness I felt in my body as a result of not being able to move. As a way to help calm me, the doctors prescribed anti-anxiety medication, which took the edge off but not completely away. Every day was a struggle to fight my fear, and my ever-increasing health challenges weren't making it easy.

A common side effect of MRSA is pneumonia, which I unexpectedly contracted in the first couple of weeks at Craig. My lungs filled with fluid and I was having difficulty breathing. Since I'd already suffered from a collapsed lung in the ICU, this development was of great concern. The fluid in my lungs made me feel as if I was suffocating. Because of my experience as a seasoned sky and scuba diver, I knew certain techniques to control my breathing and to help me stay as cool and calm as possible. But it wasn't easy when I had nurses standing over me telling me to breathe slower and into the bag they had placed over my nose and mouth to help me get control.

Control.

Now there's a thought, because sometime early on during my stay at the ICU, it hit me like a ton of bricks that perhaps for the first time in my life, I had no control over *anything*. And this was not welcome news.

I will readily admit that before I got sick I was considered by many to be a control freak. I never believed in asking anyone for help—even when I could have used it. It has never been my style and even now, something I will likely struggle with for years to come.

When I started RE/MAX, I thought I had to do everything myself. I was the chief cook, the washer, the guy who emptied the trash and anything else that needed to be done, because I had a lot more time than money back then. As I matured and hired better people than myself, I realized that relinquishing control to those who are more skilled or experienced than you is how a business really grows and flourishes. No man is an island. If you create a successful business operation, you mature with it. If you're smart, you'll let the experts do what you hired them for and leave them alone. You can't micromanage people in the boardroom or, as I have now come to find out the hard way, in a hospital room either.

Even though I knew and trusted the nurses and practitioners who were coming to my aid, I still desperately feared being alone. I begged anyone who would listen not to leave me for a minute—and for the most part, they didn't. There are a couple of times during the day when nurses change shifts. During those times, there's a gap in accessibility. Junior and Mary had been still taking twelve-hour shifts to be at my side, but as time ticked by, they both needed to get back to their lives. Mary's husband Jeff had been extremely supportive of the time she was spending away from home, and was tending to their business in her absence. These are the kinds of family situations that can sometimes take a toll on relationships if there isn't a strong foundation in place.

There were plenty of times when I tried to convince my children to go get the car, unplug me and sneak me out of the hospital. Of course, they knew I was delirious, and because I was suffering short-term memory loss, wouldn't remember asking them this five minutes later, so they usually just appeased me by saying they were going to get the car and that they'd be right back to fetch me. Then they'd leave the room, grab a cup of coffee or a bite to eat and return thirty minutes later to find me fast asleep. They described this experience like the movie *Groundhog Day*, where Bill Murray's character relives February 2nd over and over, aware of the time loop while everyone around him isn't. He used the experience to take advantage of the unsuspecting locals, playing jokes on them and learning their secrets.

My children did their best to find the humor in what was an otherwise agonizing situation for everyone. Mary came up with the idea of stocking my room with grab-and-go food that anyone who came by could take. It was set up like a virtual 7-11. Nurses who hadn't eaten a thing all day or night would pop in to check on me and grab a cup of Ramen soup, a bag of chips, Twinkies, Ding Dongs or a handful of candy to keep them going. The kids thought it was a great way to give back and take care of the doctors, nurses and techs who were taking such good care of me. I was glad to have the company when they came in, especially at night when I couldn't sleep.

MARY

Dad was constantly asking me to get him out of the hospital. He'd say things like, "We should get on the plane. There's money on the runway. We need to go. Go get the golf cart. Tell the nurses you're signing me out." At first I was confused by his desire to escape the hospital because I was certain he was aware of where he was and why he was there. I was trying to be logical with someone who wasn't in a logical frame of mind. I'd take out a pen and paper and write all of his requests down.

Golf cart, got it.

Plane, ok.

Sign paperwork, check.

Then I'd walk out the door. He was none the wiser by the time I returned.

When I was awake, the kids often made jokes, tried to get me to laugh, and generally kept me upbeat, even if I couldn't remember anything they said moments later. "Foam in, foam out" became one of their favorite sayings, because of the antibacterial foam everyone was required to use before entering and exiting my room. There was one day when a family friend thought it would be funny to bring a giant stuffed moose into my room. One of my nurses could see that I was confused by it. There's no doubt I would have gotten a big kick out of that moose if I had my wits about me. But I didn't. My nurse was able to convince my kids to take the stuffed moose to the opposite side of the room so I wouldn't start having nightmares about it. The moose became the butt of many jokes in the coming weeks. There were pictures taped to the wall of my room of the moose wearing my thoracic brace as it ate out of the giant candy bowl that had been brought in for visitors, and even one of my doctors listening for its heartbeat with his stethoscope. Those pictures made everyone laugh when they saw them. My cognitive thinking was limited at best, and though there was no ill-intent, I believe they were humored by my ignorance from time to time. I can't say that I blame them. From what I've been told, I had the mind of a preschooler and for a while there, I was acting like one. I'm sure I promised great fortunes to each of them, but I as far as I know, they didn't get anything in writing, so I believe I'm still a financially secure man.

Junior and Mary were by my side 24/7. The fact that they and so many others were there, holding my hand or talking to me even when I wasn't awake, was the emotional bridge I needed when my fear crept in.

And it always came, especially late at night.

I've always thought of myself as a tough son of a bitch. Hell, I tell people that all the time. And for most of my life, they believed me. Well, that bravado works fine with the curtains open and the sunlight shining through the windows in daytime, but it quickly disappears at one o'clock in the morning when no one else is around and unimaginable terror starts to seep into the dark places of your mind. Even with Junior in the room, my dreams often turned to nightmares that seemed so real I felt all alone.

At some point, one of the drugs they were giving me really

started to affect my mental state. As a result, I began having extraordinary hallucinations. They started when I was in the ICU and continued throughout my stay at Craig Hospital. They only came at night—never during the day.

Prior to getting sick, I'd heard all sorts of stories about guys who go into rehab and during their withdrawal, hallucinate all kinds of crazy stuff, seeing monsters, snakes and such. I always laughed and thought it was a heap of crap.

It's not.

Almost all of my hallucinations took place with me in the jungle and even though it didn't make sense, usually involved a boat of some type. They were all brilliant, vivid and felt as if they were actually happening. The most common hallucination had me in a huge gunfight with some bad guys. There were three of us on my side and dozens on the bad side. I recognized the two guys who were with me—they were police officers I'd known for years from Denver. I have no idea why they were in my dream, but I was glad they were there.

In that dream, we were in a terrible shootout where we killed almost all of the enemies. There was one guy left to kill. I could hear him moving around and see his shadow, but I couldn't get to him.

Exhausted, I leaned against one of the officers. Just then, I saw the last bad guy standing. He had a beard, was heavily tattooed and looked American. I could see that he was holding a six-shot eight inch barrel .357 Colt Python. I could smell his sweat and taste his fear. I remember thinking it was strange that he was using that kind of gun, because these days it's so obsolete.

I watched as he made a mad dash across the woods and hid behind a tree. I didn't know why he was such a bad guy or why we were fighting. It was obvious that we were in a situation where nobody could win. Either all of us died, or only one of us walked. Tired of waiting, I stood up and shouted across the forest: "Why in the hell are you trying to kill us? Why don't we call it quits? It's been a long day. Lots of people are dead. Why don't you turn around and leave?"

The stranger answered back that he had fought in Iraq and had been left behind. He felt like nobody cared for him then or after he got out.

"Brother, I've been there. I understand the pain you're going through. I've lived alone myself. This has been a hell of a day and there's no reason for anyone else to die," I answered as I threw my gun down on the ground. "Go ahead and leave. It's over."

The stranger looked at me and said, "Were you in the military?"

"Yes." I told him about my experiences and even though we fought in different wars, I knew we were brothers in arms.

"We will both live another day," he said as he placed his weapons down too. I watched him get on a motorcycle when suddenly a pretty woman got on with him just before they rode away.

"How did you know he wouldn't kill you?" one of my cop friends asked.

"He wasn't going to kill me. He was the one who was hurt and trapped," I said.

I had that same hallucination several times, which started to grow into more stories of me in the jungle. In one variation, I was tied up and being held hostage. As hard as I tried, I couldn't get loose or summon help. Another had me working for the DEA fighting drug lords, while several others took place in a hospital where I tried but couldn't get anyone's attention. I was so thirsty, but people were ignoring me. I was lying in a hospital bed, unable to move my arms or hands, crying, asking someone, anyone for a glass of water, but nobody would help me.

Finally, a nurse came into my room and asked, "What's the problem? You're making too much noise!"

"I need help. I'm thirsty and no one will take care of me. Where is everyone?" I was always panicked during this particular hallucination.

"We're busy!" she said, before turning her back toward me and walking out the door. Although all of my nurses in the ICU and Craig were extremely kind to me, the nurse in this hallucination was a real Nurse Ratched, the awful nurse from the movie, *One Flew Over the Cuckoo's Nest.*

The various hallucinations were endless, and they all had this strange gurgling sound in them that I'd hear every eight to ten seconds. I sometimes got so violent from the thrashing about, I'd pull out my IV and try to take off my oxygen mask. Whenever that happened, an alarm would go off, alerting the nurses on duty that I was without oxygen. Junior was usually around and had my mask back on before anyone could get to the room. Still, my nightly episodes were trying for everyone. The hospital wanted to tie me down, but my children wouldn't allow it. They knew that was the worst thing they could do to me because I'd feel like a prisoner instead of a patient. Instead, whenever Junior couldn't be there, they placed a technician or a nurse by my bedside all night so I wouldn't hurt myself. If I started to have a hallucination of any kind, they'd reach over, touch me and hold me until I woke up. Sometimes their face would be right in front of mine.

"Dave, you're having a nightmare. Do you know where you are?" they'd ask.

Sometimes I could answer; other times I could not.

"Dave, you're in the hospital. You've been injured and you're having nightmares. I'm your nurse and I'm sitting with you to keep you safe. You'll wake up and it will be daytime again soon. I'm here to take care of you. Don't be afraid." They always spoke in a calm, rational and kind tone.

I was terrified by these experiences. I had no control. I couldn't sit up, swing my legs over the side of the bed or stand. I couldn't turn on the lights, find the switch to call the nurse or anything else that seemed so near and yet so very far. Sometimes I'd go to sleep with the nurses call button tied to my bed rail, but even then I didn't always have the strength to get a hold of the rail, pull myself over and grab the switch. To compensate, I'd put the switch in my hand or lay it on my chest.

I'd doze off, and even if I wasn't hallucinating, I could still hear that strange gurgle in the back of my mind. Months after the hallucinations started, I began to regain my cognitive reasoning and realized the gurgling sound was actually coming from the IV pump they had me hooked up to. It would pump for eight to ten seconds and then reset itself. When that happened, it made a gurgling noise. I didn't recognize it when I was awake until one day it just hit me: That's the noise I heard in the background of every hallucination I had.

As I began to get better, the doctors took me off the pain medication that likely induced the hallucinations. They subsided, but the terror never truly went away. Once I started thinking clearly, I worried about how I would get around on my own, specifically how I would get to the toilet by myself. I worried about regaining my speech and my overall quality of life. I wasn't even sure I'd ever regain the motor skills needed to wipe or feed myself. I still couldn't hold a tissue between my fingers. I obsessed about being a burden on my family and friends, something I found terribly disturbing to even think about. I had always been the caregiver, not the care-"taker." This new role was not one I could readily accept, which would make things harder for me than they needed to be. Still, I'm the kind of man who would rather find my own way than depend on others for the basic necessities I'd come to take for granted. It was humiliating and frustrating to think that this is who I would become if I allowed it.

JUNIOR

For me to calm my head, I like to hear background noise, so I often turn on the TV. When I stayed with Dad, I kept the television on and listened to the news all night through the earpiece they give patients. I sat right next to his bed. Even though he was out of it most of the time, I'm positive he was aware of what I was hearing, especially when his delusions started. They all seemed tied into some story I was listening to on CNN, especially Operation Fast and Furious, which was going down at the same time Dad was in the hospital. Of course, they also seemed to correlate to being trapped in his bed for so long. I'm sure Dad didn't like the way that made him feel.

—— MARGARET KELLY ——

I was visiting Dave one afternoon when he asked me to hand him a tissue. I handed it to him without thinking he might not be able to hold it. The tissue slipped through his thumb and forefinger and fell to the floor. I quickly handed him another. Again, he wasn't able to close his hands with enough force to hold it. This realization brought tears to Dave's eyes. I took a third tissue from the box next to his bed and began wiping my eyes, saying, "It sure is dry in here. Isn't it?" Without missing a beat, I dabbed away the tears from his eyes and said, "We ought to get a humidifier in here. It's too dry."

These are the thoughts that come into your mind when the sun goes down and everyone has gone home. When morning came, the nurses could always tell I'd been awake all night. They could see the worry and shame in my eyes. Still, I'm a man's man who would never admit I was scared, especially to a woman. Now, that's not a sexist statement so much as it's one filled with the bravado I was talking about a few pages back. You see, the bravado returns when the sun comes up.

"Are you ok, Dave?" the nurses asked.

No matter what I said, they knew I wasn't, and they never once emasculated me by pointing out the obvious. They'd simply pull up a chair, hold my hand, rub my arms or legs and talk to me until my mind and thoughts were diverted to something positive. They knew I wouldn't talk about how I was really feeling so they did their best to help me move through it with kindness and compassion.

Once I was on the road to recovery my cognitive thinking returned. To monitor my cognitive reasoning skills, a therapist came to my room every day to ask me a series of simple questions. The first was always, "What day is it?"

I finally had my kids put the day and date on the wall behind the therapists so they couldn't see it.

"Today is Wednesday, May 16th, 2012," I'd promptly answer.

"Very good! You're coming right along!" They never once figured out what I was doing.

Around the same time, one of my nurses started talking to me about dealing with my Post Traumatic Stress Disorder—PTSD. I had no idea what she was referring to. But then I realized my psychiatrist was trying to tie my hallucinations to my time in Vietnam.

As part of my healing process, I sat with a psychiatrist twice a week. He said it was obvious to everyone there that my dreams, nightmares and hallucinations were all indications that I was suffering from my time serving in the war. I adamantly disagreed, as the hallucinations first started during my hospital stay and immediately ended when I was taken off a certain pain medication. In my everyday life prior to getting sick, I hardly ever thought about the war, and I certainly never suffered disturbed sleep from serving in the military.

Vietnam veterans get a real bum rap because society wants to paint them as damaged goods, when in fact our rate of suicide, drug abuse, alcoholism and homelessness is no different than those who served in World War II. The media created the story about soldiers who came home from Vietnam who couldn't fit into society. Sure, there were those who genuinely suffered from their experiences, but there are also some who took advantage of it and used it as a crutch. That's not unusual and it certainly isn't the first time in history it happened. I was vehement with the psychiatrist that my issue wasn't PTSD but rather the fact that I was paralyzed and handcuffed to a gurney. I was unable to move and was scared to death because I was on such heavy drugs for my pain that it was messing with my brain. If that suddenly clustered me into a lost generation, it was time to review my entire life.

Once they took me off of that drug, the hallucinations stopped and my world began to slowly come back into focus. I'd still wake up in the middle of the night, but at least I knew where I was and the reason I was there, and though there were still moments filled with fear, given my circumstances, they were reasonable and to be expected.

I was clearly getting more and more like my old self—and I liked the way that felt.

CHAPTER 9

Just 10 Feet

"What lies behind us and what lies before us are tiny matters compared to what lies within us."

-Ralph Waldo Emerson

The last prescription my doctors gave me for pain was one hundred and fifty tablets of morphine. He told me it was better for me to live through my pain—to learn to use it as motivation to move, build muscular strength and to stand up again. After four months of being flat on my back in hospital beds, most of my muscles had atrophied. I had no quads, glutes, abs or framework of muscles to support my spine. If I had a prayer of getting back on my feet someday, I would have to start by building enough strength to support each of those muscle groups just so I could sit up on my own.

When my physical therapy began, the techs had to use a lift to get me out of my bed and into a wheelchair. The lift had a yellow tarp, which they would slip underneath me. I had to roll onto it so they could wrap the remainder of it around my body. There were straps that came up between and outside of my legs with another two that went over my shoulders. The lift itself dropped down from the ceiling above my bed or exercise platform where

I would have my physical therapy and daily exercise sessions. They would snap the lift to each connection point on the tarp and slowly raise me into the air until they could position me into my wheelchair. This same device was used every time I needed to be placed on or taken off a therapy table and in or out of my shower chair.

At the time, the use of the lift was excruciatingly painful for me, especially on my lower back. I told my doctor that the lift hurt my back and made it feel worse than before my surgery. He reluctantly told me it would be that way for six to eight months. I had no choice but to get used to it.

As a way to help alleviate some of my discomfort, the doctors ordered a custom brace that wrapped around my back and chest to see if that would make moving any easier for me. It helped, but it certainly didn't make it less painful. I used the brace with a chest plate for about two weeks while I worked on strengthening my core muscles. As I slowly grew sturdier, I graduated to using the lift without the brace, which was still painful but no longer unbearable.

I made my stay at Craig a personal competition against myself. I pushed my body harder than any of the therapists would have, especially in the beginning. They were experts in dealing with patients who needed to be inspired, driven and pushed hard. They had no idea how to handle my level of commitment when I came along. I remember the first time they placed me in my standing chair, a wheelchair that has a plate that drops down and locks you in place so you don't fall out when they crank the chair into an upright position. Your knees and legs are like vices in those chairs. The seat slides up so you can stand straight. Your total body weight is on your legs but you can't fall because you're locked in from the body plate. I knew it would be painful to use, but I wasn't afraid. If I could conquer this exercise, I'd be allowed to move on to using the robot machines—the ones that physically move your legs to help teach your muscles by example how to move the proper way again.

"How long do I have to stand in this chair before I can use the robot machine?" I asked.

"Twenty minutes."

"How long does everyone usually stand on their first try?"

"About a minute or so."

"I'll make the twenty minutes the first time," I said, full of audacity and conviction.

"Dave, nobody has ever done that. It's impossible."

"I'll make it. I'm all about making the impossible possible," I said. And I meant it, too.

Before we started the exercise, I thought back to my training as a jet pilot. While flying jet planes, you use a pressure suit that expands when you start to build G-forces during aerobatic maneuvers. The suit pushes blood out of your legs and chest, back into your brain so you don't pass out. The pressure suits work to about 9 G's, but some aerobatics I learned took me to 13-15 G's. In flight school, I was taught to hold my glutes, abs and quads as tight as can be, as if you're sitting on a toilet while constipated, and to push as hard as you can. That extra pressure pushes blood into your head so you stay conscious. Once you know how to do that you can call upon it in times of need.

I had been flat on my back for several months. I was barely sitting up in bed on my own and my blood pressure hadn't yet regulated to become stable. Doing this exercise over time was a way to improve that. An ordinary standing person shouldn't have an issue with blood flow. However, if you've been lying on your back for any extended period of time, the changes to your body are immense. The blood starts draining out of your head much quicker, which means you are prone to fainting. This is one of the reasons I had to be monitored all of the time. The hospitals are scared to death of a patient fainting, falling and getting hurt. The techs were watching me very closely, especially as the one minute marker turned to two, then five then ten. So when they placed me in the standing chair, I didn't fully understand the danger I was flirting with as they cranked me into the full upright position.

"Are you ok, Dave?" the tech asked.

"Get me all of the way up here. Let's go!" I said as I began doing my own exercise to push more blood into my brain.

"Dave, whatever you do, please don't faint. Tell us if you're going down!"

I thought I was going to make the full twenty minutes, but at fifteen minutes and twenty seconds, I had to give up.

"Ok, put me down. I'm about to faint and throw up." I conceded.

My failure and my queasy stomach bothered me for well over an hour, but then I got over it and asked if I could give it another try tomorrow.

"Not until we talk to your doctor!" they said.

The techs were initially scared by my will and determination. A typical patient would take four or five weeks to work their way up to fifteen minutes in the standing chair. They agreed to let me try again but on the condition that they monitor my blood pressure every three minutes. I nailed the twenty-minute threshold the very next day. Surprisingly, my blood pressure didn't vary a single point the entire time—probably because I was squeezing and pushing blood into my brain, but they didn't know it.

Body part by body part, I was trying to get back to where I could stand and then walk on my own. After four months, my catheter had become rather uncomfortable. With all of the hard work I was doing, it was also getting in the way. The biggest concern about having a catheter in a man for so long is that the bladder gets weaker and might never come back to full function—meaning, I might not ever be able to urinate on my own again or worse, have any control over this bodily function. Sympathetic to my discomfort, the doctors agreed to remove the catheter to see where I was at. Believe me, removing the catheter is just as uncomfortable and painful as inserting it. The good news is, I peed like a champ. I was able to void as much urine as I was holding in my bladder every time I went. The bad news was that I didn't have a lot of control over my need to go and my ability to hold it, so in the beginning, I occasionally wet myself. I was terribly humiliated and embarrassed the first time this happened because I missed my first Lokomat session as a result. A Lokomat is an automated treadmill where the patient's legs are guided according to a pre-programmed physiological gait pattern. It helps make the leg muscles stronger and promotes more muscle mass. I hated that I kept all of the Lokomat therapists waiting while a nurse had to clean me up. I swore I would never do that again—wet myself or keep the good-hearted people who were there to help me heal waiting. I was respectful of their time, just as I wanted them to be of mine.

I spent the next several weeks working on my balance, strength, muscle-building and movement exercises. The therapists were extremely kind and cooperative with my demanding physical expectations. My overall physical therapy routine was designed to get me to that next step where I could attempt to start walking on my own. They tried to be extra cautious with me, but I wouldn't allow it. I wanted to push harder, make quicker progress and give one hundred and fifty percent of myself each and every day. It got to the point where they finally gave in and said, "Go ahead and do what you want because we know you're going to anyway." And they were right. I pushed them to push me—which has been a common theme througout my life. Everything I have ever done has been about pushing others as a way to push myself harder and to reach for a higher standard.

I wasn't willing to stay disabled. I wasn't ready to accept that I might not walk again. I wasn't choosing that life. I was choosing to do whatever I could to avoid it. I reminded everyone that I was one tough guy who could take whatever they asked me to do as long as it brought me closer to my goal. I wanted to walk again—the sooner the better.

I was still obsessing over what it would mean to walk just ten feet. Ten feet meant I could have a perfect life. I could get out of bed and take two steps to sit in my chair. I could get out of my chair and take two steps to sit on the toilet. I could take my chair to the car and not need a handicapped van. If I could walk ten feet, it would be the impetus to walking twenty. If I could walk twenty, then I could walk a mile. To me, ten feet meant freedom and independence.

Some patients at Craig were just like me—gung ho and willing to try anything to make their life better by improving their health. Others didn't have that drive. Many of the patients there were young, immature and had never been given the chance to succeed at anything in their lives. They tell their therapists they don't *feel* like doing an exercise because it hurts too much. They refuse to cooperate and as a result, stay exactly the same each day. Though the physical therapists and techs do their best to encourage them to participate in the program, each of us is there of our own free will. They can't make us do anything we don't want to do.

JUNIOR

Dad has always been black and white about everything he does. He's all in or he is out, so you never have to question where he stands on things. When it came to his rehabilitation, he wasn't going to give an inch in his fierce determination. He would keep working as hard as he could until he hit the point of exhaustion or someone else stopped him from hurting himself. I'd attend his therapy sessions and would watch other patients come in asking if they could cancel because they really wanted to go back to bed and watch TV. Not Dad. He'd do his session and ask for an additional half hour. He would struggle through every grueling minute and refuse to quit. I don't think I've ever witnessed my dad quit at anything he set out to do—and I knew for sure, he wasn't about to start now. He always said, "Small failures, amazing achievements." He was willing to do everything necessary when a lot of other people would have given up. He had an unstoppable, bear-down-and-get-it-done attitude that was a constant affirmation of how strong he really is.

The next milestone in my pursuit of mobility was learning to do a pivot turn. I knew that simple turn on my feet held the key to the kingdom. One day my doctor came into my room and said he wanted to get me from my bed to my chair so he could examine me. He was busy reading my chart when I suddenly swung my feet over the side of my bed, stood up and pivoted before sitting down. I had visualized the move over and over, believing I could do it—and I did.

The doctor caught my unexpected move out of the corner of his eye. "You can't do that!" he said with about as much authority as he could muster up.

"Oh, really?" I responded before standing up, pivoting and sitting back down on my bed again. I pulled the sheets up over my legs as if to say, "Says who?"

"You see that board on your wall? That says you still need a sliding board to get out of bed. Until it says otherwise, that's what you're supposed to do."

"I don't like the sliding board. It hurts my butt." And it did. My backside was still very sore from my flap surgery and I wasn't allowed to wear underwear yet because it rubbed against the backside area they repaired. My bare skin on the slide board made it very challenging to gracefully, let alone gingerly, get out of bed. I needed to grab onto something to tug myself up off the board, which made the move much harder than it needed to be. I had learned to pivot by using the Lokomat and knew I finally had the leg strength to pull it off. I had spent three weeks practicing until I had it down.

"As long as these instructions are on your wall, that is what we will follow."

"Aw, Doc. C'mon. That's written way up there and I can't

see a damn thing without my glasses."

He just shook his head in disgust. "You're going to do whatever you damned well want to do, aren't you?"

"Yes, sir, I am." I knew what I was capable of doing and what my limitations were. I wasn't being defiant so much as determined. I had fought full contact karate for five years. I wasn't afraid of hitting the ground. The doctors, nurses, therapists and technicians want to make sure their patient doesn't get hurt during the healing process. The last thing I needed was to stumble or fall, break a leg, twist my ankle or hit my head and risk another staph infection. Falling is their number one concern. Not trying harder was mine.

Every doctor, specialist, nurse, physical and occupational therapist, tech and others at Craig kept telling me I was working too hard. Hell, I've been hearing that my whole life, so why stop now? Besides, is there such a thing? So I asked one of my doctors how much exercise is *too* much.

"Dave, I know you. You're committed and are always going to the wall with whatever you do. Screw anybody who is going to tell you not to do something. Do as much as you can tolerate. Be real with how you feel before, during and after. One morning, you'll wake up and say you don't feel like exercising that day. When that happens, don't. It's your body telling you it needs a break. I know it will be totally against your goals and the expectations you've set up for yourself, but it's your body's way of saying time out. That's when you'll know it's time to take a day or two off. Knowing you the way I do, those two days will make you angry and upset, but use that time to reset your goals and go back at it with a vengeance. Listen to your body. Don't listen to anyone else."

This advice came at the perfect time. I knew I could be a frustrating person to work with because I always wanted more than my therapists were going to let me have. By doing this, I also accomplished more than they believed I could. I never missed a single therapy session and always wanted to do more than they scheduled. If we were doing something twice a week, I wanted to do it three times a week. If they asked me to do ten reps of an exercise, I did twenty. If they had me lift twenty pounds, I told them to make it thirty. I wanted the reputation that I tried harder than anyone else, and did everything I could to earn it. In this case, more was definitely more.

Once my balance was stabilized and my backside was finally healed to the doctor's satisfaction, they suggested it was time for me to try out my power chair. Up until this point, I had been pushed around in a regular wheelchair by one of nurses, therapists or techs. When I heard the words, "power chair," I conjured up an image of one of those scooters I've seen elderly people moving around in. I thought, "Cool, a little power chair to zip around in, because I'm going to be walking any day now."

No one had given me false hope. I was the one dreaming big. I was the only person convinced I would walk out the front door of Craig all on my own. When we got to the power chair, I tried to keep the smile on my face, but I couldn't, because I realized it was just a sped-up motorized wheelchair. My whole body sagged at the sight of it. Until that very moment, it had never occurred to me that I might be in a wheelchair for the rest of my life. The thought never even crossed my mind because my well-cultivated, step-by-step attitude had kept me so positive. First I'd be on crutches, then I'd be walking and before you knew it, I would be hunting and fishing again just like I used to. No one ever said I might actually be confined to a wheelchair. Ever.

I was devastated.

Why didn't someone tell me this? I had been daydreaming of running around a track like Carl Lewis or Usain Bolt, the fastest man in the world, just to prove to everyone they were wrong. I thought my wheelchair was just a temporary but necessary step I had to accept until I could walk again. A horrible feeling of fear and defeat took over my entire body. And they knew it. They kept trying to talk to me in a cheerful and pleasant manner.

"We don't like to refer to this as an electric chair, you know, for obvious reasons. It's a power chair, Dave," someone said. I think they were trying to be light, but I wasn't amused.

They placed me in the chair and began to take measurements, from the width of my behind to the depth of my seat so they could customize *my* power chair. Woo Hoo—not. It might as well have been an electric chair, because at that moment I thought I could die.

When I got back to my room, one of the nurses asked me why I was so down.

"No one ever said the word wheelchair to me. Does this mean I'm going to be in a wheelchair for the rest of my life?"

"Dave, we don't know. Every injury is different. We can't be certain if you will take one step or you'll walk a mile. But this is how you're going to learn to survive." She was doing her best to be honest, but I wasn't happy with what I was hearing. I wished she had said something like, "Your rehab is going to take you months and maybe even years. In the meantime, you need to get from spot to spot and because of the paralysis on your right side. You don't have the ability to use your arms to push yourself along. You'll have to maneuver around this hospital for months, and this is your chariot. We'd give you a car if we could, but we can't. This is the closest thing we can offer until you take that next step toward walking with crutches or using braces."

I don't know why my version felt more positive and full of hope to me, but it did. The reality is I could have spent the next several months daydreaming that I would move my legs and take one step at a time, and then ten steps, and then, miraculously, I'd be walking that mile. If you look at goals from a long distance, they can appear hard, if not impossible to achieve. But, inch-by-inch, it is a cinch. You accomplish one thing, and then another. You still have weakness, but you've worked hard every day to get stronger. I'm not saying that sheer will and fierce determination is all it takes to heal. Sometimes, you won't heal. But your frame of mind certainly matters. If I had let the power chair take over my emotions for more than a moment, it could have proven to be a damaging setback. But I didn't have time for setbacks. I had to keep looking and moving forward.

To be certain, the power chair was a rude awakening, but it was something I eventually came to love.

I know, surprising, right?

My power chair actually made getting around the hospital a lot easier for me throughout the rest of my stay. My physical therapy sessions were in various buildings, wings and floors around the facility. Each session lasted anywhere from a half hour to an hour. I always wanted to work right up to the very last minute, which meant I needed to leave like a bat out of hell to my next appointment. My chair made it so I could get to and from those sessions quicker without giving up any of my time with the therapists.

By the beginning of June, it was clear I would not be going

home by the goal date I had set of June 27th. The doctors assured me I was making giant strides in my recovery, and if I would agree to give them three additional weeks, I'd be that much stronger when I left Craig. They reasoned that if I stayed three extra weeks, I would likely have a much better long-term response to the rehab. I still couldn't walk, sit on the toilet or even turn over in bed without help. I was determined to get there, but I wasn't there yet.

"Dave, you can do anything you want. You are not a prisoner here. But if you'll give us three more weeks, we can take you so much further and you will be safer, more comfortable and less of a burden on people at home." The doctor's logic made perfect sense to me.

I wasn't happy about it at first, but I agreed that I was making very positive progress. If three weeks meant I would be more stable, less reliant on others and able to leave as a stronger man, I was willing to reset my going-home goal date to July 17th.

As a condition of the additional three-week stay at Craig, I negotiated six one-day passes so I could go home for six-hour visits each weekend during my remaining time there. Luckily, my house had already been built to accommodate Gail and her mobility challenges. The hallways were wide enough for a wheelchair, the shower in her master bathroom had bars on the walls and was big enough for a shower chair and our house staff was already well acquainted with the proper way of helping Gail around the house. As for me, the men on our staff are strong and well built. They had no issue picking me up out of my power chair and placing me wherever I needed to go, whether it was an armchair in the living room or my bed. Even though the team of professionals didn't approve of the way the guys moved me around at first, I was fine with it. I've never had an issue being handled, especially after spending so much time in the very capable hands of my caregivers at Craig. One of my nurses was adamant that Mary and Junior learn to do certain things before she could feel good about my decision to be home on the weekends. I was ok with Mary feeding me, and Junior helping if I had a bladder accident. But I was also struggling with the idea of casting my children in the role of caregiver. I didn't want them to have to do anything for me. I wanted to do things for myself. I certainly had no desire to become an added responsibility in their already busy lives. As it was, they'd given up six months of their free time to be by my side. Learning to accept help of any kind was a hard lesson for me. My fear of becoming dependent kept me motivated enough to keep working harder, but it didn't make it any easier to ask for help when I needed it.

All throughout my stay at Craig, Dr. Gary Maerz, my lead doctor, came to see me early in the mornings at least five or six days a week. He listened to my heart, thumped my chest and used his stethoscope to check my breathing. He had read the nightly report, talked to the nurses and kept up with my day-to-day progress. He has a terrific bedside manner. He is the kind of doctor who isn't afraid to show compassion or affection. He'd often hold my hand and ask, "Are you ok? Is the pain management working? Are you comfortable?" He showed great concern for me throughout my time there. The last question he asked before leaving my room each day was, "Do you have any questions?"

One morning, I looked him square in the eyes and said, "Yes. I have a question. I've been here for fourteen weeks and I haven't heard anyone talk to me about the Twelve-step program or having to give up drinking the rest of my life."

Dr. Maerz looked confused. "Dave, you're in a spinal cord and head injury rehab center. This isn't an alcohol or drug rehab." I had to dig my fingernails into my thighs to keep from laughing. I looked at him with a straight face and said, "Really?" And then put my head down and pretended to go to sleep.

Concerned, Dr. Maerz went to the nurse's station and repeated what transpired.

"Is he serious?" he asked one of the nurses.

The nurses all started laughing. "He plays jokes like that on everyone. He's yanking your chain, doctor." And of course I was. I knew exactly where I was. But, as they say, laughter is the best medicine!

I spent the next three weeks working harder than ever. I didn't want to move my going-home date for a second time. I felt I had made enough progress to attend our annual company barbecue that was being held at Sanctuary Golf Club. I didn't tell anyone I was planning to go except a couple of the nurses and therapists at Craig. I had them arrange for a special wheelchair-friendly van to pick me up and drive me to the club.

MARGARET KELLY

I had no idea Dave was coming to the barbecue. No one did. It's always a great event, but his surprise appearance would make 2012 simply unforgettable. We set up a lot of outdoor games and activities, so most of the festivities are held outdoors. I looked over and saw a van pulling into the driveway. Just then, I received a text from Dave that read, "Surprise! I am here."

I saw him getting out of the van in his wheelchair as he made his way over to see everyone. It blew me away. I grabbed the microphone and called everyone back into the pavilion.

"Can I get everyone's attention please? I have one additional announcement to make. I forgot to tell you that we have a surprise visitor." Dave rolled in on his wheelchair, smiling from ear to ear. Everyone there gave him a standing ovation. He got tears in his eyes, just as we all did. It was just so emotional. What a treat to have him come and see everyone.

I was extremely happy to see everyone at Sanctuary and was overwhelmed by the response they all had when they saw me. For most of the people there, it was the first time they had seen me since I'd fallen ill. I wasn't physically the same, but I'm certain they could all see I was mentally as strong as ever. Being there that day was a very important step in my journey. Although I knew Margaret had done her best to quash rumors and keep membership informed of my progress, I was worried about what the people in our company might be thinking. There was no better way to show everyone my progress than to be at the barbecue. Some of my caregivers were worried I wasn't up to the trip.

Others thought it was the best motivation to keep me inspired. The latter folks were right. I came back feeling better, stronger and more eager to keep taking those baby steps toward healing.

FROM THE DESK OF MARGARET KELLY

6/21/12

Hello everyone,
Many of you have asked or wondered about the condition of Dave Liniger, who's been hospitalized in Denver for several months.

I'm pleased to report that Dave made an appearance at Sanctuary Golf Course yesterday during the annual RE/MAX Headquarters summer barbecue. It was a real treat for HQ employees to see him, and when he spoke to the group it was quite a moment. Everyone had a chance to say hi to him, and we all had a wonderful afternoon. He looked great and was thrilled to be there.

Dave continues to progress in his recovery from a staph infection and several resulting surgeries on his back and neck. He's doing physical therapy exercises for several hours a day, and though he'll remain in the hospital for another month or so, he's able to make weekend visits home now. He's really happy about that.

Dave is dealing with a lot of physical challenges, and the healing process will take time. But he's very much the Dave we all know – sharp, optimistic, pushing himself, refusing to quit, and eager to tell a story. He's hopeful about the days ahead, and committed to doing whatever it takes to get better.

Gail is doing fine, surrounded by family and support, and all the Linigers continue to thank everyone for their concern and prayers. As I've noted before, please don't send flowers, cards or other gifts. They know how much you care.

If there's anything you need from the team in Denver, please let us know.
Sincerely,

Margaret Kelly

Margaret Kelly
Chief Executive Officer
RE/MAX World Headquarters

On July 16th, the day before I left Craig Hospital as an inpatient, I sat down with my physical therapist to have a real heart-to-heart conversation.

"Privately and confidentially, what are your thoughts about when you think I might walk again? I know the doctors won't promise anything and I'm aware there's a chance I might never walk on my own, but you know how hard I've been working. I have worked harder than anyone you have ever met, so please tell me the truth."

Before I allowed her to answer, I thought about what I was asking her to do. Most people think they want to know the truth, but sometimes the truth can hurt. I learned a thousand lessons from my days in the military, but one of the biggest occurred when I got passed over for a promotion. I went in and sat down with the Major and asked his permission to speak freely.

"I've made every promotion before this one. What did I do to make you pass me over this time?" I was sincere and curious.

"Dave, you're not part of the team here. You don't play on the softball team. You don't come to the Friday afternoon cocktail hour for a beer and you show no interest in being around the other guys in your troop."

I was stunned by his response because in addition to being in the service, I was taking college courses and was holding down three part-time jobs so I could buy and sell real estate on the side. I worked at a gas station, a movie theater and delivered newspapers to 7-11 and Circle K every morning between 2:00 and 6:00 AM. I wasn't like the other twenty year olds who were partying and having a good time. I was trying to build something with my life.

When I explained this to the Major, he said "You're trying to build it on your own, with no team. If you're always standoffish or never have the time to enjoy a drink with your comrades or attend a company picnic, people will assume you don't want to be around the rest of us. Either you think you're too important or too good. Whatever your reasons, it doesn't work here. We're the military, son. We live and die together."

Here I was, thinking I was sending a message that I was an extremely ambitious and hardworking young airman who was really going places in his life, and the message they were receiving was that I was a standoffish, snobby son of a bitch who didn't want to be around the rest of the guys. You can bet I never missed another gathering, and was never passed over for another promotion. The truth stung a bit, but it was exactly what I needed to hear.

So as I prepared myself to hear what my physical therapist was about to say, I realized I might not like it, but I needed to hear it, just as I needed to hear the Major years ago.

"Dave, just bust your butt. With hard work and your same level of perseverance, we hope you'll be able to walk by Christmas. You still have a lot of muscle you need to replace and you don't have a great sense of balance yet, but you'll get there. It takes time and patience. I'm not stupid. I know you're going to go home and try to get up and walk. But if you come back here with a brain injury caused by a fall, I'm going to be very disappointed in you."

Trying to lighten the mood, I looked at her and said, "I have thick cushioned carpeting."

She wasn't amused.

I went home that night extremely disappointed. I was deeply discouraged by her Christmas prediction because I wanted to be on my feet much sooner than that. But at the same time I respected her for telling me her honest opinion.

The relationships I forged with my nurses, therapists and technicians at Craig were second to none. I loved the guys like they were my brothers in combat and the women were all lovely, beautifully spirited ladies. The techs assigned to me had to do the dirty work no one else would ever choose to do, and yet they were there with a smile every day as they happily changed my sometimes soiled bed sheets, helped with my bathroom needs, cleaning, bathing, showering and anything else I need assistance with along the way. They were all amazing people, doing their best on behalf of others. In many respects, they were exactly the type of individuals I have always sought to be around.

The RE/MAX attitude has always been that you play better golf with better golfers. When the competition is intense, you can't be a slacker. You try to play up to the best in the game you're playing. It's part of my DNA to surround myself with the very best people in everything I do. Successful companies like Apple, Microsoft and RE/MAX aren't built by one man or woman; they're built by a team of incredibly talented people who have a shared passion for a cause they believe in. Simply stated, I couldn't have recovered to the extent I did without each and every one of my caregivers, who all kept me competitive and committed. It would be a huge understatement to say that these relationships are close; they're intimate. These fine people become extremely involved in your life, and as a result, you become involved in theirs too. I feel as if I've forged world-class friendships as a result. I will never forget the work we did together—and their patience, kindness, understanding and willingness to put up with me even when I was a pain the ass. I'll never forget the support they extended to help get me through the worst period of my life.

There was no way to predict that I would emerge as the lucky one, with enough strength and determination to someday recover most of my body functions. No one can heal for you, but these professionals do their best to help you get as far as you can. It was much better having a support team cheering me on in this way than a group just saying, "We hope you will be ok." Every day I heard encouraging words such as, "You're looking good," "You're getting stronger," and "Keep working hard and you'll be perfect again." Those words certainly got me closer to my goal. Without those fine men and women, I would not have recovered as I have.

On July 17th, my first day home after being released from the hospital, Gail had invited fifty or so of our friends and their spouses to a Welcome Home party celebrating my progress. By the time I got there, I had already put in a long day of physical therapy and exercise at the hospital. I was exhausted. It was seven o'clock when the first guests began to arrive. It was also around the time that the special hospital bed I had ordered arrived. I needed a bed with sides because I still couldn't turn over on my own if I didn't have something to grab onto, and I didn't want to worry about falling out of bed at night either. Unfortunately, they delivered a bed that didn't have sides. Next, the oxygen tank I ordered showed up, but the machine they brought was broken. The one that worked was unfamiliar to me, so I had to learn how to use it. And then the nurse came to teach me how to clean and change my IV three times a day. I had to flush it with saline solution and then sanitize it with alcohol before putting it back in within ten minutes of taking it out. Once I did that I had to flush the line again, tighten everything and make sure the connections were made. I was trying to learn all of this while a party in my honor was going on.

Before I got sick, I could multitask anything. I could give a speech to thousands of people and solve large-scale business problems before breakfast on most days. But my first night home proved to be too mentally taxing for me. I was completely overwhelmed. I had never felt like that in my life. I couldn't see anybody after that. I decided to put myself to bed and just rest. It was strange to be home. It's the one place you're supposed to feel safe, secure and worry-free, yet on this occassion it made me anxious, worried and stressed. I didn't want to admit it, but the doctors were right. I wasn't physically ready to be home yet. I actually looked forward to getting back to Craig and starting my outpatient work.

CHAPTER 10
My Next Step

"Every day, think as you wake up...
Today I am fortunate to have woken up. I am alive. I
have a precious human life. I am not going to waste it.
I am going to use all of my energies to develop myself, to
expand my heart out to others, to achieve enlightenment
for the benefit of all beings. I am going to have kind
thoughts towards others. I am not going to get angry,
or think badly of others. I am going to benefit others as
much as I can."

-Dalai Lama

Unfortunately, I didn't *walk* out of the hospital on July 17th. But I did spend the next two months working as hard as ever, continuing my physical therapy sessions as an outpatient five days a week to help me get stronger every day. By August, I was able to walk four feet using a walker. That gave me the freedom to go from my power chair to the toilet, shower and my favorite comfortable chair in our family room. I will admit, there are a few dings and scratches around the house from my attempts to move around. In fact, just as my nurse suspected, I even took a few falls along the way. Thankfully, I didn't hurt myself too badly or

I think she might have killed me. The positive outcome of falling was that I discovered I had the ability to get myself back up all on my own.

By late August I had a real handle on using the walker and was able to transition to crutches. I once had beautiful, muscular calves, but now they just didn't have the strength to hold up my body mass. My therapists were very cautious when I began using the crutches, for fear I might fall again. They placed a safety belt around my waist, flanked me on both sides and held me up until I got the hang of using them by myself. It didn't take me long.

On September 6th, I hosted a party at Del Frisco's Steakhouse in Denver to say thank you to my family, friends, colleagues, and the primary doctors, nurses and therapists who helped me get back on my feet. There were a hundred or so people there, which was amazing for me to see. Over the course of eight months, so many new faces had become critical in saving my life. Some I remembered; others, especially those from Sky Ridge, I didn't. I was unconscious for most of my stay there, so I couldn't possibly recognize those nurses. But that lack of recognition didn't diminish my utter appreciation for the work, time, energy and effort they put in on my behalf.

I told the hostess of the restaurant that after everyone was seated, I wanted to make a speech. I was looking forward to having my first drink in eight months that night—my favorite, a rum and Coke. But I also had something else planned. I whispered in her ear, "When I'm done speaking, I'm going to use my cane and not my crutches to turn and walk to every table in the room." The only other people who knew my plan were Junior and Adam. We practiced my moves for two weeks in the privacy of my basement at home. I started off by using one crutch at a time, walking around and around until I felt comfortable enough to use just my cane. It was a covert operation, as I wanted to surprise Gail with my progress. We always practiced whenever she wasn't home. I knew she would be blown away when she saw me walk. I couldn't think of a better way to let her know what an inspiration she had been to me.

I sat while making my speech and naturally got very emotional. I thanked everyone in the room for being there that night and throughout my illness, and expressed my deepest appreciation for their patience along the way.

"For everyone's information, I have my big boy panties on for the first time since January 29th—and if you haven't noticed, I'm wearing slacks and a shirt!" I smiled, thinking about the day one of my therapists—a female ex-Marine—yelled at me and said, "C'mon, boy. Man up and put your big girl panties on!" I'd never heard that expression before, but I loved it and haven't stopped using it ever since. I'd spent eight months in a hospital gown, robe and sweats. It felt good to be dressed and even better to be out with my family and friends like old times.

When I finished speaking, I handed the microphone over to the hostess, stood up, took my cane and began to walk. Everyone gasped and then began to applaud. Some even cried tears of joy as I slowly made my way across the room. I kept my eyes on one of my therapists, who had a hunch I was up to something before this. For several weeks leading up to this moment, she kept warning me not to do anything crazy. I promised her that I wouldn't try to walk with a cane before she said it was ok. Oops. I lied. I had never broken my word to her in the past, but I felt it was important to show everyone who was there that I defied all odds—that I could walk. She was watching me like a hawk. When

I got to her table, I sat down next to her and asked, "Are we ok? Will you still be my therapist?"

"Don't try that again for a while, Dave, ok?"

"You have my word. I promise I won't do it again. But just remember, if I fall down, we now know I won't break."

CHUCK

Dad sent me a picture of himself standing on his own. When it came through on the cell phone, Bonnie and I were having coffee and it took our breath away. We didn't know if it would ever happen. He had a big smile on his face. I consider it to be a miracle of sorts and yet, I also know my dad was on a mission. He won't ever give up until he meets whatever goal he has set. I grew up watching him tackle everything he does with that same commitment and perseverance. Even now, he has more energy than I do. I don't think that will ever change. It is an incredibly amazing feeling to see what he has gone through and witness this kind of recovery.

She hugged me and said that even though she was proud of my accomplishment, we ought to go back to the crutches for a while. I didn't have the heart to tell her I had started driving too. No one gave me permission, but then again, no one ever took my license away from me. As long as I have braces on my legs, I've got the strength and ability to press down on the gas and brakes. I've got the mobility in my arms to steer, and the mentality of a professional racecar driver who isn't afraid to be behind the wheel. I would never do anything that would endanger others—I may endanger myself along the way, though. After all, I'm still a guy who needs a little adrenaline in my life, and I have a lot of adventure left in me.

When people hear my story of survival and healing, many ask how this experience has changed me. It's reasonable to think that going through this kind of life-threatening challenge would bring even the most macho guy to his knees. But for me, it didn't. Aside from the physical manifestations, I am pretty much the same man I was before I became ill. While I might concede that I'm more aware of the needs of others as a result of this experience, I came into it as a practiced caregiver, making sure my wife had everything she needed to make her life comfortable and safe throughout the years, and helping so many of my close friends face challenges of their own.

A lot of people talk about the moment they face their maker and begin to barter, plead, and wheel and deal for more time.

"If you let me live, I will be a better person.

I'll give more to charity.

I'll spend more time with my family.

I'll be a better spouse.

I won't work as hard.

I'll take time to smell the roses.

I'll go to church more."

And so on....

I never had that conversation with God. I never once thought about how I would live my life any differently than I was already living it. Mostly because I was living exactly the way I wanted to, already doing those things as part of my daily existence. I don't look back on my life with a single moment of regret or remorse for things I didn't do, should have done or might have done differently.

Most people mature and change as they get older. Young kids in college start out naïve and idealistic. When you have life experiences, they impact your perception and the palette you draw from, which ultimately changes your perspective and future experiences of the world. My palette became expansive. I always wanted to be a man of many worlds, and I am. I have been a soldier and I have seen combat. I am a husband and father. I have been a policeman. I have been a businessman. I am a philan-thropist, an explorer and adventurer. I have had all of these titles but never once let them define me. These are just pieces of the man, not the whole of who I am.

I can't tell you why I'm alive. I suspect that part of the reason was the unshakable faith I had—the belief that I could live through anything and that this too would pass. But I don't really know if it was positive thinking that got me through, or if it was the fact that I was stronger and tougher than anyone else who'd battled this kind of infection. Maybe it was because I'm just that one in a million who got very lucky. Although I'm not a religious man myself, I know that there were many people praying for me.

When I found out that Margaret had blessed me with holy water, I later joked with her that I was surprised there weren't burn marks where she crossed my forehead. We both laughed aloud when I said that!

I'd heard about messages on the RE/MAX Facebook page,

where thousands of agents from around the world sent me their well wishes, thoughts and prayers. On one hand, my thought was "Tell them to pray for my enemies. I don't need help—my enemies will, if I live through this!" But of course I was just being funny. The truth is, I deeply appreciated every single good thought and prayer that came my way.

Gail and I have lived a fabulous life. We have a wonderful family, homes, cars, boats, horses and everything we could ever want. In fact, we have more than we need. For the past ten years, we've made a conscious decision to give back as a way of showing our appreciation for all we've been given. We agreed to divide our income into thirds. The first third off the top goes to charity. We support many great causes, including two that are especially dear to the RE/MAX organization, Children's Miracle Network Hospitals and Susan G. Komen For the Cure.

Gail and I became involved with Children's Miracle Network Hospitals (CMNH) in 1992 when we formed a partnership with them to raise money for the amazing things they do for sick or injured children and their families. Our RE/MAX friends in Canada introduced us to this very worthy cause. Children's hospitals often lack the means to buy the latest equipment or help children who have no funds or insurance. Most hospitals won't turn anyone away, so the money CMNH provides over and above what they get from insurance companies and from federal government assistance really helps the hospitals provide for those in need. We were so encouraged by the work CMNH does that we decided to make it an official RE/MAX charity. Thousands of RE/MAX agents and brokers contribute in all sorts of creative ways.

Each year, we invite a CMNH Miracle Child to our annual R4 convention. During the opening session, the child appears on stage and tells one of our officers his or her story. It's always very inspirational. We also hold an auction offering all kinds of interesting items and packages—from golf outings at Sanctuary to precious jewelry—to raise money. During one convention, a lovely young lady named Mallory joined us as the Miracle Child. She was just seventeen years old, and even though she'd been born with several severe health conditions, she was eagerly looking forward to starting college in the fall. Ordinarily, I don't bid in the auctions because people say it isn't fair to go up against me when they want something. During this particular auction, however, there was a pair of beautiful, high-quality diamond earrings on the block. It took me a while, but I eventually outbid everyone. I took the diamonds up to Mallory and handed them to her.

"They're yours. Put them on." It was a magical moment for me to see Mallory light up and shine even brighter than those diamonds.

Another year, we featured a teenager who had a passion for racing like I do. At the time I was heavily involved with NASCAR. Rick Carelli, one of my favorite drivers and a friend for more than twenty years, agreed to donate one of his fire suits to the auction. The bidding got hot and heavy, but I ended up buying it. When they handed me the fire suit, I gave it to our Miracle Child that year.

I've thought of moments like that, and of other Miracle Children I've met over the years, a lot during my illness. Spending so much time in the hospital myself has really put into perspective what these kids and their families go through. These children are real heroes, and it makes it especially rewarding to know that RE/MAX has been there for them.

In October 2011, Gail and I were honored on behalf of RE/MAX at the CMNH annual convention, in part because

RE/MAX agents had donated more than $100 million during the twenty-year relationship. It was a huge honor. RE/MAX has always had a culture of giving back to the communities it serves. And this was an easy cause to support. One hundred percent of the money raised for CMNH stays in the local community. I'm very proud of our association with CMNH, and of the generosity our RE/MAX family displays every year.

Another cause dear to my heart is Sentinels of Freedom, an organization devoted to helping men and women of the armed forces who have suffered severe injuries. Wounded warriors have always been important to me. I've raised money for Fisher House, which provides housing at military bases for families of wounded soldiers so their loved ones can be there to help support them throughout their recovery. I bought the original CNN Hummer at a charity auction and sent it to dozens of high-profile events around the country, including the Kentucky Derby, the Daytona 500, the Detroit Auto Show and the Balloon Festival in Albuquerque to help raise awareness about Fisher House and to solicit donations. Millions of people have seen the Hummer, and millions of dollars have been raised as a result.

I even took an under-the-radar trip to Walter Reed Hospital in Bethesda, Maryland to visit the soldiers recovering from injuries there. I solicited the support of the Denver Broncos, who donated jerseys and footballs and sent players and cheerleaders from the team to accompany us on our visit. It was an incredible experience to see the spirit of those warriors, who are coming back as double-or even triple-amputees, looking forward at the world, trying to make the best of what they have left. It was very inspirational to me, and something I often thought about after I got sick. My visit with those warriors then was as a former military man. Today, I'm a recovering soldier just like them. I look forward to making another trip there someday very soon.

What do we do with the rest of our money?

The next third goes to Uncle Sam and the final third to our family.

When we started RE/MAX, it was not an easy undertaking. Like many small businesses, we struggled a great deal. For a long time the paychecks were few and far between. The officers who joined the company early on have stuck with me from the very start. They never wavered from their commitment to me, nor did I to them. As a result, many of my very closest friends today happen to be colleagues—both past and present. Of course, we've made a big success from following our dream, but in the early days there were no certainties or guarantees of that. One of the promises I made to those loyal friends from the start was that RE/MAX would never become a family business—meaning my children would not come in and take over senior officer positions because they came from the lucky gene pool.

When my kids were young, we were not wealthy people. We were like any other normal middle-class family. I never believed in spoiling the children or giving them more than they needed. They all had jobs when they were teenagers, which taught them to work hard so they could buy their own cars and other things they wanted. This kind of life experience helped them develop a good work ethic from an early age. They quickly figured out they couldn't be two minutes late or call in sick to go to a party with their friends. As a result, each grew up with tremendous discipline and appreciation for the things they earned. I had many long discussions with all four of my children when they were young, explaining that they couldn't count on RE/MAX to make their living as they found their own way in life. Those conversations continued as they became adults. While I would not let them work at the company, I agreed to pay for their college educations and to even invest in business ventures with them if they made sense. But for the most part, they've been raised to be independent, to be on their own in business and in life.

CHUCK

Something changed for me after Dad got sick. My perspective on the importance of family strengthened. It wasn't like I had ever been distant from them, but seeing Dad struggle and watching how our family and friends rallied around him opened my eyes and made me want to be closer to everyone back in Colorado. Since this happened, Bonnie and I have decided that being around our family is much more important that anything we have as far as our businesses and jobs. It is not just for my dad. It is about my entire family—my sister and my brothers are my best friends in the world, and I can't think of anything that is more important than being together as a unit.

One of the things my children have spoken to me about over the years was my absence in their lives as I grew RE/MAX into the business it has become today. Before I got sick, our relationships were good. All of my children have been very close their entire lives. They are good-hearted and well-intentioned in all that they do. They take care of their mother (my first wife) very well and have always shown Gail a great deal of love, respect and support throughout our years together.

When I got sick, it took the level of our relationships to a new high. I will never be able to thank my children enough for coming together to support Gail and to help protect me. Moreso, I am so proud of them for the way they conducted themselves with others throughout my illness. One of the nurses, who I became very close to, told me that everyone was nervous when I first arrived at Craig Hospital because no one knew what to expect. All they knew was that there was a confidential patient who was a large donor to the hospital over the years. While you might think that would have gotten me special privileges along the way, I assure you, it didn't. My status meant nothing to them. Craig, like any top hospital, doesn't care if you have a dollar to your name or if your name is on the wing you're staying in. What this nurse most wanted to know was whether my family members and I were going to be demanding pains in the butt. I can certainly understand where she was coming from, as nurses are often targets for angry patients and families. Remember, I was once that guy—the one who didn't trust nurses after Gail's accident. I'm sure my reputation preceded my arrival!

I'm told that within hours, my family and friends had completely won over the hospital staff. They were the kind of group that jumped in to see how they could help the nurses, technicians and other hospital personnel instead of hinder them. So often, families get in the way of what needs to be done. Trust me, this doesn't do anyone any good—especially the patient. When families argue, disagree and pull power trips about who is going to be in charge and make decisions, it's hard to make the right choices because egos are involved. Calm minds always prevail.

This was also true for me throughout my stay at Sky Ridge and Craig. I knew I was a tough son of a bitch before I'd gotten sick, but my seven months in the hospital taught me that I wasn't as tough as I thought. Even in my weakest moments, I always did my best to show the people who were helping me a great deal of courtesy and to extend the same kindness they were giving me. After all, these were the people helping me get well, and that still means a great deal to me.

I'm not perfect. I've had more than my share of enemies and have made more than my share of mistakes As you mature, you try to fit into the world more comfortably, to not be confrontational or hurt people, and you do your best to always show your appreciation. That is why I wanted to write this book. It's my way of saying thank you to those who walked along my path on my journey of hope and healing. But it's also meant to be something more. You see, the idea of this book first came to me when I was in the ICU. I thought about all of the people going through a crisis in their lives without the kind of love and support I had throughout my illness. I saw patients in Craig whose families couldn't be with them for financial reasons or because they had other obligations keeping them apart. I was fortunate that I could go through my rehabilitation near my home. Most patients don't have that luxury. As I spent so many nights awake and scared, I desperately wanted to find something I could read to help me understand what I was going through. I wanted a book that inspired me to keep working hard and to motivate me to never give up. I hope this is that book for you.

This journey is far from over. When I look at the things I've lost, they really aren't that important. To a certain degree, I have lost my ability to use some of my right arm and hand. I have a weakness that is never going away on the right side of my body. I am never going to pass the annual FAA flight physical to be a pilot. But that's ok, because I can still fly. Maybe not like Superman—yet. As you know by now, when it comes to this old lion, never say never.

As I put the finishing touches on this book, the holidays have come and gone. My goal to be walking by Christmas has been met—sort of. Today, I'm able to walk on my own for a short time first thing in the morning. I still use my cane to keep me steady and safe. By the afternoon, I find it easier to get around on my crutches. By the end of my day, which is as full as ever, with going to the office, continuing my physical therapy and even traveling a couple of times a month, my body is tired. I have no problem giving in to that fatigue and sitting in my power chair for relief. I am still in pain, but have learned to deal with it. I will likely spend the rest of my life on antibiotic therapy for the staph infection, which still resides in my body. And I will continue to work hard, doing everything it takes so that one day I can finally toss that cane in a corner as a reminder of where I once was, where I've been and what is possible.

When I look at my life, I realize that despite the challenges, Gail and I have been pretty damn fortunate. I'm not ready to write my obituary yet, and I don't know exactly what's coming next. What I do know, though, is that many dear friends and family members love me—and they made it possible for me to get through the past year. Despite all of the things I have, that love and support is what truly makes me a wealthy and very lucky man.

FROM THE DESK OF DAVE LINIGER

7/25/12

Hello everyone,

As many of you know, I've been dealing with significant health issues since late January, when I went to the emergency room with a terrible pain in my back. It turned out to be a serious staph infection that had invaded my spine, and I've had several surgeries to address the problem. As a result, I've spent the past six months in several hospitals; the first eight weeks in Intensive Care. To say the least, it was a very close call.

What I wanted you to know today is this: I'm out of the hospital now, and have returned to work.

In other words, despite any rumors you may have heard, I'm very much alive.

I've stayed current with what's happening at RE/MAX and in the industry, but there's nothing like being back in my own office, at my own desk. It's great.

My plan is to work most mornings. In the afternoons, I'll be doing physical therapy five days a week, on an outpatient basis.

The PT is focused on helping me regain full movement in my legs and arms. I'm using a wheelchair for now, but the doctors are optimistic about my chances for a full recovery. I certainly expect that to happen, but it will take time.

I want to thank and compliment our CEO Margaret Kelly, her staff, and the Region Owners for doing such an outstanding job in leading our organization this year. In fact, the entire team at HQ has been terrific. Everyone has been extremely supportive of Gail at a time when she and my children were under a great deal of stress.

I also want to thank you all for your prayers, thoughts and kind gestures. I've never once felt like I was in this thing alone, and for that I'm truly grateful.

My PT schedule will keep me in Denver for the time being, but you can count on me being in Las Vegas for R4 next February. I can't wait to see you all there.

And, once again, thank you for everything.

Regards,

Dave Liniger
Chairman and Co-Founder
RE/MAX, LLC